W9-BFX-747

MOLAS

FOLK ART OF THE CUNA INDIANS

Other books by Ann Parker & Avon Neal

Ephemeral Folk Figures: Scarecrows, Harvest Figures and Snowmen

Rubbings From Early American Stone Sculpture

MOLAS

FOLK ART OF THE CUNA INDIANS

ANN PARKER & AVON NEAL

Photographs by Ann Parker

BARRE PUBLISHING
Barre, Massachusetts
Distributed by Crown Publishers, Inc.
New York

First published, 1977, in the United States by Clarkson N. Potter, Inc.,
a division of Crown publishers, Inc. All rights reserved under the
International Copyright Union by Clarkson N. Potter, Inc. No part of
this book may be utilized or reproduced in any from or by any means,
electronic or mechanical, including photocopying, recording, or by any
information storage and retrieval system, without permission in writing
from the publisher.

Clarkson N. Potter, Inc.
A division of Crown publishers, Inc.
One Park Avenue
New York, New York 10016

Published simultaneously in Canada by
General Publishing Company Limited.
Printed in Japan by
Dai Nippon Printing Co., Ltd., Tokyo

LIBRARY OF CONGRESS CATALOGING IN PUBLICATION DATA
Parker, Ann.
    Molas: folk art of the Cuna Indians.

    Bibliography: p.
    1. Molas.   I.   Neal, Avon, joint author.   II.   Title.
F1565.2.C8P3 1977   746.9   77-21739
ISBN-0-517-52911-4

This book is
dedicated
to all mola-makers
of the San Blas
Archipelago

The Cuna's Paramount Chief, Nele Kantule, of Ustupo, visited the Canal Zone in the early 1930s. There was a traveling circus in town, and when he saw an elephant for the first time he was stirred to say, "There are things easier to understand than the reason for such an animal."

CONTENTS

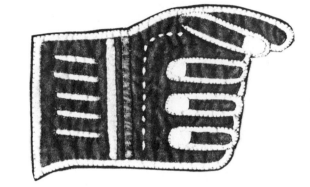

INTRODUCTION

Women clothed with the sun.
   A movable feast of walking pictures where we may read the symbolic language of earthbound man and man in space. The sun-drenched families of red, orange, and yellow which suffuse the unchanging dress of the Cuna Indian women reflect the spoken and unspoken history of the mythic past and inventive present.

Why molas?

For someone like myself who saw his first molas on the island of Ailigandi twenty-five years ago, a fine mola is to me as fine, as beautiful, as visually exciting as is much of what I love and admire in the arts of the past and present. They astonish and surprise. They are like transcriptions by Liszt whose variations on a theme are often more brilliant than the original source of inspiration. They are curious and evocative in their juxtapositions of fact and fancy; often puzzling, often cryptic, and sometimes unfathomable. Within their predetermined format (the panel size of the blouse provides the discipline and their technique), they ring infinite changes, much like a bell-ringer who scatters his sounds to the world at large.

   Today the term *folk* is challenged and supplanted by *ethnic* or *primitive, popular* or *naïve*. The confusion among

CAT ON CUNA STOOL

BALSA WOOD CARVING OF
CUNA WOMAN

specialists should not color your response to what a mola is. A mola is a blouse and a work of art. Like other creations, there are good molas and bad molas. The choice is yours, made easier by the magnificent selection throughout this book.

Fashions in art, dress, and aesthetics rise and fall with the tides. The art and construction of a style of dress is in no way inferior to that of painting and sculpture. Good design remains good in any media, and the test for me of a design's validity is how far one dare go in enlarging the original. I see the molas as translations into frescos, mosaic murals, and, most exciting of all, as stained-glass windows. In another context, the molas are filmic images documenting the life and times of our world.

They transcend the circumscribed political, national, and geographical tags which were pinned on all folk art by pedants who could never find the right pigeonhole. It has been a kind of intellectual security blanket that prompted the classification of the fine arts as superior to the decorative arts. Major and minor. Their inequality has been clearly a definition of the trained professional as against the unschooled amateurs whose primary function was to make things of use. If they were beautiful, so much the better; but as they were made by anonymous hands, so much the worse for considering them as works of art.

Of course, I am writing of the past. Students and teachers of art history, curators and museum directors, scornfully dismiss this view as academic nonsense. Or do they? Have you seen a permanent or even a temporary exhibition of molas in your local museum or gallery?

There is nothing random or anarchic in mola designs. They require the freedom of forethought no different from the architect's precisely lined blueprint. The strictures inherent in the construction dictate a consciousness of imaginative technical expertise and application. These are not innocent-eyed splashes of color. They encapsulate a vocabulary of motifs, encyclopedic and alchemical, turning the dross of found objects, advertising, and comic books into golden perceptions.

Their designs evoke the labyrinthine arabesques of the Irish *Book of Kells* and the symbolic patterns of Mochica, Paracas, and Nazca cultures of Peru. It is a Cuna human comedy, an eternal circus peopled by the extraordinary, the colossal, the gargantuan parade of a never-ending spectacle. An insatiable appetite for life. They may also be read as dream images observed and recorded with the calculating intuition of a Hieronymus Bosch, Francisco de Goya, or Max Ernst.

If they are considered as Pop Art, then the molas of the Cunas are the quintessence of the derivative. If they are looked upon as *kitsch*, as vulgar, as popular art at its worst, or best, then they epitomize the total iconography that surrounds us in our civilization. A fearsome burden that does not deter the women from producing a colorful procession of subjects, year in and year out.

One other fact becomes an image of enchantment. I can think of no other culture in which the pictorial art of a society has been dominated by women. This collective genius contradicts everything that we in the West have glorified in our cult of the individual, the authenticated original whose value in the marketplace depends on the right signature. In our culture there have been numerous artists and craftswomen whom one can name. The profound difference between them and the Cuna Indian women is that the Cunas maintain a continuing style, a homogeneity of vision and visual effects. We are never

BALSA WOOD CARVING OF
CUNA MAN

11

RCA VICTOR MOLA • *This is a fine example of one of the first great mola designs to use a trademark for its inspiration. Numerous versions appeared during the 1950s, reflecting the Cunas' love for both dogs and phonographs. The lettering, which is only slightly jumbled, reads* RCA VICTOR, HIS MASTER'S VOICE, *and the* PERRO MUSICA *below is Spanish for "dog music." This marvelous design is dealt with in some detail on pages 240 and 241.*

12

concerned with who did which mola, and the signature which does not exist is of no importance.

"The eternal footprint" of the Cuna women can be seen in each mola worn or made for sale. It is a trademark as distinctive as any they have transformed, modified, reinterpreted by a mythopoeic imagination which no longer exists in our world of predigested facts and interpretive statistics. Perhaps their kind of understanding survives only with those men and women who can neither read nor write. Such skills as we take for granted seem to be superfluous to those whose joy of expression and sense of humor is always at their fingertips.

Before the blouses are turned into mail-order substitutes of conformity, I would urge you to visit the islands. When I bought my first mola, it was love at first sight. My love has not diminished by a single stitch. I hope that love will also come to you through the fond eyes of two other mola lovers, Ann Parker and Avon Neal, celebrators of their friends the Cuna Indians of San Blas.

Brooklyn, New York   CARL FOX
April 1977

PRIMITIVE RCA VICTOR DESIGN
• *Although badly conceived and crudely worked, this RCA Victor trademark still has a charm of its own. If a mola design catches on, it is usually copied over and over again. When this happens, an image often degenerates as the preceding artists' mistakes and confusions are accentuated. Letter forms gradually become unrecognizable, and in the end a copy may bear only a passing resemblance to the original.*

13

PREFACE

Four lively elements came together to make this study irresistible for us: molas, Cunas, the San Blas Islands, and our love of a challenging quest.

We saw our first molas nearly twenty years ago when Carl Fox exhibited some prime examples at the Brooklyn Museum's folk art shop. We were amazed at the graphic design and incredible color combinations. A closer inspection revealed stitchery that appeared so impossibly flawless that it seemed beyond the scope of human workmanship. And, not least, we were charmed by their amusing content—they had a fresh wit and humor that belied the naïve presentation. Mixed in with dazzling abstract patterns were images right off Madison Avenue . . . only better.

Two designs from that first show were especially memorable, a beautiful "His Master's Voice" trademark and a whiskey bottle, its colorful label meticulously duplicated right down to the smallest lettering in fine needlework. There was also a Kools cigarette ad, a primitive airplane, a rooster playing a guitar, several familiar cartoon characters, plus wonderfully conceived flora and fauna. It was a feast for eyes too long battered by the crass visual assaults of modern advertising.

Shortly afterward the artists, Estelle and Carl Ashby, showed us their fine collection of molas and turned our folk art interests in the direction of Panama and the San Blas Islands.

We soon concluded that molas were among the most exciting and important art forms being created in our time. All the searching and researching we've done during the intervening years has confirmed that early impression. We have found these beautifully appliquéd panels infinitely varied in imagination and artistic expression, a unique body of contemporary folk art surpassing all our greatest expectations.

Once we began traveling in the San Blas Archipelago and came to know the Cunas, we responded to them and their way of life with empathy and some curiosity. We have found these people physically and spiritually beautiful, combining intelligence and dignity with friendly warmth and playful wit. They have consistently made us welcome, taken us into their homes, and treated us with deference and kind consideration. We have accepted their hospitality, slept in their hammocks, eaten their food, and endured with them many of the rigors of *cayuco* travel among the islands. Some have become our friends and aided us greatly in our quest for mola art. Had there been no molas at all in San Blas, the hundreds of memorable moments we have shared with Cunas of all ages would have made our trips to their country more than worthwhile.

The paradisiacal San Blas Islands have cast an ever-deepening spell over us since our first dawn flight across the mountains from Panama City in the early 1960s. Each subsequent journey to this hauntingly beautiful coast has drawn us deeper into its magical way of life.

POLYCHROMED *UCHU* WITH BEADED NECKLACE

15

WOOD CARVING, MAN WITH FISH

It was the quest as much as anything else that kept leading us back to San Blas, the search of the folklorist seeking out the artifacts that add up to some part of a people's cultural heritage, the hope that the next encounter will produce some startling work of art that must surpass all others, the expectation of more and better molas in the next village. We were eager to know as much as we could about this art form and the people who made it.

Over the past dozen years we have looked at tens of thousands of molas in Panama, the United States, and other countries. The variety seems boundless, and each time we thought we had discovered the best example of a particular design another came along which was better. We finally decided that Cunas were making molas faster than we could look at them.

We have been bold in our speculations about individual molas and the origins of their design, interpreting them according to the information we acquired most often from mola-makers themselves. The search for sources of motifs can be most frustrating and unrewarding until one day when least expected an answer leaps out from the pages of a back-dated magazine or from a nostalgia era package label. Sometimes it was puzzling when the Indians offered different explanations for the same design. Even more confusing were the attempts to seek symbolic meanings in every mola motif. In the end we drew our own conclusions and hoped we had not gone too far astray.

We must apologize for any errors we have made in our suppositions; the subject is vast and sources have often been lost or obscured by design manipulations. We are not the first nor will we be the last to stray off course in our efforts to decipher designs that may be perfectly obvious to someone else. Unraveling the scrambled lettering on molas is somewhat like playing multilingual anagrams.

For at least a decade we have been hearing that the art of mola-making is dead and only inferior products for the tourist trade come out of the San Blas Islands now. We don't find this to be true at all. In fact, good molas are even better now than some of the earlier ones based on similar themes. Many of our best molas have been purchased within the past five years and have been created since 1970. To be sure, there is a proliferation of inferior work, but that is understandable since the demand is greater and Cunas are as capable as anyone else of equating time with money. Mediocre molas find homes as readily as those of superior quality, mainly because the majority of buyers are not qualified to judge the differences and indiscriminate buying is bound to cause an overall lessening of quality workmanship. Mola design and detailing are, in general, considerably less subtle now than they were a few years ago as rickrack, machine stitching, and other hurry-up shortcuts are used much more frequently. However, an art form can continue to flourish at its higher levels while at the same time degenerating as a whole.

Our observations have led us to believe that the great flowering of mola art came after World War II during the period between 1950 and 1965 when the Cuna imagination expanded and beautiful molas seemed to turn up everywhere. The impact of this golden age can still be felt in the excellent work being produced by hundreds of Cuna artists who take pride in their needlework and have the decided advantage of all that has gone before. As long as this tradition prevails, the art is neither dead nor dying.

The finest collections of modern molas are in the hands

WOOD CARVING, WOMAN WITH PIPES OF PAN

of private collectors. A few museums have accumulations of earlier specimens filed away in their ethnology or textile departments, but, in general, curators were not inclined toward building substantial collections of this unusual work while the best of it was still available. Now such quality pieces are widely dispersed in private hands or beyond the means of current museum budgets.

Our purpose for bringing together this material into book form is to acquaint more people with mola art; to categorize a selection of fine examples which can instruct and guide future collectors in making their own decisions; to set a standard for judging mola content and quality; and, finally, to share the incomparable beauty of these unique blouses.

We would like to thank all the people who have been helpful to us in preparing this work. We would particularly like to extend our gratitude to three private collectors: Elizabeth Hans, Sam Hilu, and Carl Ashby, each of whom generously allowed us to photograph some of their superb molas for this book.

We are also grateful to Diana Baker, Leah Barkowitz, Rose and Carl Fox, Sonia and Tony Gargagliano, Betsy and Ron Johnson, Anita McAndrews, Flory Salzman, Mr. and Mrs. Sanchinelli, Ellie and Fred Seibold, and Mary and Jim Stewart, all private collectors who permitted us to use their molas for this book. We appreciated the help that the British Museum gave us and thank both it and the Smithsonian Institution for allowing us to include examples from their collections. The Panamanian Tourist Office and their representatives both in New York and Panama were kind and helpful; our thanks go to Nieves Alba, Bill Freed, and particularly to Audrey Kline. For memorable and informative discussions about molas, Cunas, and folk art we thank Mary Black, Cheril Bruce, Yvone Gonzalez, Paul Hollister, Suni and Royce Hubert, John Mann, Anita McAndrews, and Mr. and Mrs. Carlos Zelenka. We also want to express our thanks to Johnny Alvarado and Carlos Mendez of Rio Sidra; Luis Burgos of Nalunega; Julio Coleman and Euladio Richards of Ailigandi; Rauliano Martinez of Mulatupo Sasardi; Jeronimo de la Ossa of Achutupo; and all the other Cunas who have befriended us over the years.

Our warmest gratitude goes to Sonia and Tony Gargagliano and Ellie and Fred Seibold who gave us quiet places to work, housed, fed, and encouraged us on our numerous hectic trips to New York. We appreciate all the help given us by the staff of the Haston Free Public Library in North Brookfield, Massachusetts who hastened our research by responding kindly and promptly to all our frantic requests for books. Last, and certainly not least, we want to thank our editor, Carol Southern, for extending deadlines and guiding us through the mazes of publication.

North Brookfield, Mass.   ANN PARKER AND AVON NEAL
April 1977

19

CUNA INDIAN SETTLEMENT, BAY OF SAN BLAS • *This lithographic print was made from a photograph taken in the early 1870s by a member of the Selfridge Expedition sent out from Washington to seek a practical route for a ship-canal across the Isthmus of Darien. The San Blas Islands have changed so little since then that this same scene could have been recorded in the 1970s.*

DESCRIPTIVE NOTES: SAN BLAS & ITS PEOPLE

In brief: *La Comarca de San Blas*, or the San Blas Reservation, was declared an independent state in 1925 and legally set up in 1938. It includes a narrow strip of land along the eastern coast of Panama and all the offshore islands (see map on page 242). There are more than 365 islands in the *Comarca*, approximately one-half of which lie close to shore and over fifty of these have communities on them. The remaining islands, grouped farther from land, are uninhabited, but some are used for coconut plantations which are tended for several days at a time by families in a rotation system. These islands are protected from the ocean's fury by a long barrier reef.

The land rightfully belongs to the Cunas, but governing offices are set up on the island of El Porvenir where the Panamanian *Entendiente*, or governor, resides. He oversees the chiefs of each village, pays their salaries, and is the connecting link between them and the Panamanian government.

The San Blas Archipelago is a chain of idyllic tropical isles, most of them bare except for a few swaying palms and clusters of thatched-roof bamboo huts crowding sandy beaches. They lie within sight and easy distance of the lush green jungle covering the mainland's mountain

A NOTE ABOUT THE WORD 'MOLA'
• *The word* mola *(moh-lah) means 'clothing', 'dress', or 'blouse' in Cuna dialect, but through constant usage (or, more appropriately, mis-usage) it has come to mean simply the single panel of a Cuna woman's appliquéd blouse. It is also used as 'mola blouse', which is a redundancy, like 'rice paddy'. We recognize the proper terminology but, allowing for changes in language and as a convenience to our readers, our decision has been to use 'mola' as it has passed into common usage, as a textile panel.*

21

EARLY TWENTIETH-CENTURY PHOTO-
GRAPH OF CUNA GIRL • *This photograph,
published in a 1913 book,* Panama and the
Canal, *shows a Cuna Indian girl posed
against a studio backdrop. The blouse she
wears is much fuller and longer than later
styles, and its loose, abstract pattern is
similar in concept to the early molas illustrated on pages 54 and 55.*

ranges. There is no fresh water, so inhabitants, using
dugout canoes, make regular trips up the rivers to get their
daily supply. These breezy atolls have remained free from
malarial mosquitoes and most other insect pests and, until
recently, the encroachments of modern civilization.

Explorers named the country Darien and called the
offshore islands the Sambalees Isles, from which the name
San Blas is thought to have derived. They are best remembered for having provided safe havens to pirate ships during their numerous attacks along Panama's golden coast.

The Indians of pre-Columbian Panama were probably
Caribs and it is believed that today's Cunas are descended
directly from them. When Spanish explorers first visited
the Isthmus early in the 16th century, it is estimated that
there were more than 200,000 Indians, but that number
was drastically reduced over the next few years by the
Spaniards' attempts at subjugation. Those early meetings
with the white man ended in disaster. Stories of atrocities
passed into legend and in later years Cunas favored the
English and helped them in their battles against the
Spanish.

Balboa came into contact with the Isthmians during his
famous journey in 1511 when he first sighted the Pacific
Ocean. For a while his relations with the Indians were
cordial and he was given a chief's daughter to wife. In
time, however, the greed and arrogance of the conquistadors proved too much for the natives and they rebelled.

Bloody battles raged for many years with the Indians
retreating deeper and deeper into the mountainous jungles
where the invaders dared not follow. There they set up
villages and continued to harass their enemies. But the
Spaniards had won; building settlements, they gradually
usurped the land. Pirates came and went, settlers came and

17TH-CENTURY PRINT, DARIEN INDIANS

TWO 17th-CENTURY PRINTS FROM WAFER'S AC-COUNT • *Lionel Wafer's book relating his adventures among the natives of Panama was first published in 1699 and illustrated with engravings of the Darien Indians. Aside from the artist's classical treatment of anatomy, the details conform to the author's text. As noted, the men wore earrings and gold noseplates, the earrings persisting until fairly recent times. Weapons, basketry, necklaces, penis covers, feathered head-dresses, a council house, and coconut palms, among other things, are sketched in fine detail, as are ham-mocks and robes made of native cotton. Wafer de-scribes the tobacco-smoking ceremony portrayed above, which continues to this day in a somewhat modified form. The only thing wanting in these views is a glimpse of traditional body painting designs which were the precursors of today's molas.*

23

CAYUCO FACING NEIGHBORING ISLAND AND MAINLAND • *The Cuna word for boat is* ulu, *but* cayuco *is more commonly used. Most of these cumbersome dugouts were roughed out of mahogany logs in Colombia, towed to San Blas by traders, and exchanged for coconuts. When this seagoing workhorse is eventually finished, it can be paddled, powered by outboard motor, or sailed like the one seen in the background. Beyond the tiny hut-studded island, and barely visible through an overcast sky, lies the mainland with its lush, jungle-clad mountains which provide sustenance for the area's Indian population.*

24

stayed, and in time the Isthmus became one of Spain's richest colonies. The Indians withdrew and history passed them by. The result was that they sealed themselves off from the world and remained fiercely independent. It is only during the past forty years that they have begun to accept the white man's civilization.

In 1680 Lionel Wafer, an English surgeon who had cast his lot with a shipload of pirates, was injured by a gunpowder explosion and abandoned in Panama. The Indians of Darien, who by then had already been subjected to Spanish rule for nearly 150 years, took him in, and he spent several months living among them. While his wounds healed, he learned much about their lives and customs and later published a book relating his adventures. He was a good observer. His chronicle provides the most vivid picture of early-day Cunas and has been much drawn upon by subsequent writers. This and other published accounts (of journeys to the Isthmus) inspired attempts at settlement by the British, but Spanish rule continued until its colonial hold was broken in the early 1820s. In the 17th and 18th centuries the coast of San Blas became a favorite haunt of pirate ships which hid out there replenishing water supplies from the numerous mainland rivers.

Throughout the 19th century, whaling ships and Yankee traders visited, and there are records of Cuna men signing on as sailors and traveling to far corners of the world, as a few had done earlier with pirate crews. Missionaries were also on hand, but whether their efforts were rewarded is not known.

The Cunas have a common cultural heritage. They are a tightly knit tribal society which has remained strong as a unit because of its self-imposed isolation, its refusal to

UCHU, CARVED WOODEN FIGURE

25

CUNA WOMAN SWEEPING • *Sweeping is routine in Cuna households. The space around the huts as well as the hard-packed earthen floors inside are swept regularly with simple twig brooms.*

SAN BLAS ISLAND VILLAGE AT DAWN • *By daylight a Cuna village has come to life. Here is a typical thoroughfare shortly after dawn. The windowless huts are built so closely together that thatched eaves often touch and foreigners, considerably taller than Cunas, have to stoop in order to pass between them. Passageways are kept neat and orderly, always freshly swept with a surface worn smooth by the soles of countless bare feet.*

permit intermarriage except in rare instances, and because it has imbued each generation with Cuna customs and a strict code of morality.

Today the Cuna tribe is made up of four groups divided by geography. The contemporary molas portrayed throughout this book come from the San Blas Cunas who inhabit the islands of the San Blas Archipelago and several coastal villages. The other three groups are the Cuna Brava who live in the center of the Darien jungle, the Bayano Cuna who live in a dozen or so villages on the Bayano River, and the Colombian Cunas who live in three villages across the Colombian border. The population of the latter three groups together totals only about 2,000, whereas the San Blas population is over 23,000. Within the tribe, Cunas call themselves *Tule*, a dialect word meaning "the people," and their land the Tule Republic. They use the word *Cuna* to refer to the dialect they speak.

Cunas are among the world's shortest people, reputedly second only to pygmies. Both sexes are straight and muscular with well-developed shoulders. The women possess the typical square build of many South and Central American Indians. In spite of sturdy appetites and excessively starchy diets Cuna men are seldom fat. They move with the easy grace characteristic of many agrarian and fishing people. They have straight glossy black hair which in some children turns brittle and reddish due to a certain diet deficiency. Their skin coloring is predominantly a rich bronze, although it can vary in tone to a chocolate brown. The well-known exceptions are the albinos who are towheaded and have weak eyes and very pale skin. San Blas has the world's highest incidence of albinism, a condition which has been much studied by anthropologists and others.

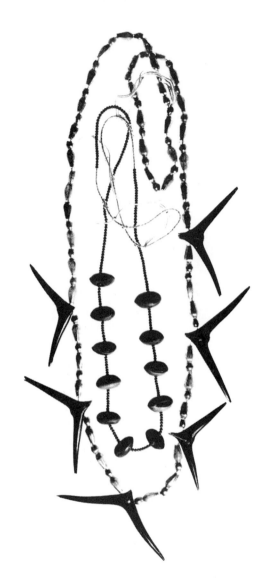

Cunas speak their own dialect, which in recent years has become increasingly peppered with both Spanish and English words. Schooling is not compulsory, but about half the children attend classes conducted in Spanish by Cuna teachers.

About 150 years ago most of the Cuna Indians who had lived in isolated jungle villages since Spanish times moved from the mainland to the chain of low-lying coral islands stretching along Panama's Atlantic seaboard. Historians suggest they did so partly to escape the torment of pestilential insects. Although their living habits changed, they remained dependent on the mainland for food and water. This brought about a further dependence on the *cayucos*, or dugout canoes, which they carved out of mahogany logs and learned to operate with great skill.

Today the Cunas farm garden plots and tend fruit trees on the mainland and grow yucca, rice, bananas, maize, mangoes, papayas, and citrus fruits. Their major crop and principal source of income is the coconut which is sold to trading boats operating out of Colombia.

Cuna society is matrilineal, with property rights passing through the female line. Early marriage is the rule. Women select their husbands, and parents make all arrangements. At an appointed time the prospective groom is taken by surprise by his men friends and carried, as though against his will, to the bride-to-be's hut, where he is placed in a hammock beside her. If he leaps out and flees he is pursued, recaptured, and returned to the girl's hammock where he may remain or escape once more. If he runs away a third time, the marriage is off. If he stays, the couple must keep each other awake by talking through the night (if one falls asleep it is a bad omen), and having done this they are considered wed. The new husband goes to live in the house of his wife's family. Marriages are usually consummated in some secluded jungle bower where the newlyweds are able to spend a few hours alone together. Divorce, although not common, is easy; the man simply takes his few belongings and moves out.

San Blas is autonomous, having gained independence after a brief skirmish with Panamanian police in 1925. Each island is governed by elected chiefs called *saylas* who officiate at nightly meetings in the council house. They make the laws and settle disputes and are paid a small monthly sum by the Panamanian government which varies according to the population of their village.

There are different kinds of medicine men who practice witchcraft and herbal cures, charging fees for their services. *Kantules* are the respected historians who keep the tribe's oral history alive by chanting it. *Neles* are the mystics who can see the spirit world and make predictions. Each of these leaders in his own way exerts an influence on mola-makers.

The Cunas' material culture reflects tropical sea island living and their houses are ideally suited for this undemanding environment. They are rectangular one-room structures, built by the men over sturdy post and pole frameworks. The windowless walls are made of bamboo stakes, and the peaked roofs are thickly covered with palm frond thatch. They are dim and airy on hot days and protective in the cool nights. The interiors are sparsely furnished with chunky stools, low tables, and primitive cooking utensils. Articles of clothing, including molas, neatly turned inside out, are hung from the beams and rafters. Large woven baskets are used for storage as belongings and food must be protected from rats. Drinking water is stored in clay jars which are partly buried in the

THATCHING • *When new housing is needed, Cuna men work together to build sturdy huts with wooden frames and bamboo siding. When all the beams and rafters are secured they thatch the roofs with palm fronds. This man is tying down the thatch with strips of pliable vine while two others place it into position from the outside. A well-made roof of this type will last for years.*

earthen floor. Some dwellings have fire pits, but most families have separate cooking huts in which hardwood logs smolder constantly to be fanned into flame when preparing food. Eight or ten family members sleep in individual hammocks strung in a row across the room and drawn up when not in use. Dwellings are communal, and family members wander in and out without knocking. Flimsy outhouses shared by several families are built over the water and furnished with large containers of fresh water and calabashes for cleansing.

One of the Cuna's most essential possessions is his dugout canoe, sometimes painted with brightly colored designs, which he uses for fishing, frequent trips to the mainland, and interisland transportation. At one time the men carved out their own boats from local mahogany trees, but now they are purchased, already roughed out, from Colombian traders who bring them on order for the Indians to finish in their own time and manner. These cost anywhere from $50 to $100. Some of the more affluent can afford outboard motors and purchase them alone or communally, but most still rely on paddles and crude sails sometimes made of flour sacking.

Tools are simple but efficient. The heavy-bladed machete is used for everything from digging in the earth to hacking wood and cleaning fish. It is, in fact, the implement that makes the Indian a jack-of-all-trades.

Clothing, except for the women's colorfully appliquéd blouses, is undistinguished. The men wear American-style shirts and trousers, the older ones, black fedoras, a custom picked up from their contacts with the outside world. The women wear wraparound blue printed cotton skirts made of commercially printed yard goods acquired by trade, and bright red scarves with yellow patterns

TYPICAL ISLAND SCENE WITH COCONUT PALMS • Community activities are carried on in the shade of coconut palms which grow in wild profusion on some of the less densely populated San Blas Islands. Children make a playground among the dugouts which are hauled ashore between fishing and interisland trips. The ground, which is only a few feet above sea level, is flat and sandy with little vegetation. In this typical San Blas Island setting, sailboats can be seen in the background and mainland mountains are visible in the hazy distance.

HEAVILY POPULATED SAN BLAS ISLAND • *During the rainy season leaden clouds hang low over the entire San Blas area, with streaks of sunlight breaking through occasionally illuminating the islands with a haunting silvery light. The boat traveler approaches a barren-looking island rising from the sea and is faced by what appears to be a jagged band of cliff. As the distance narrows, the scene slowly changes and it* *becomes apparent that the soft brown line is a row of closely packed bamboo huts dotted with brilliant blossoms. Upon arrival, the boat traveler sees that these bright splashes of color are molas hanging on lines or fences, laid out on roofs to dry, or adorning Cuna women as they flit among the dwellings.*

covering their cropped hair. They also tightly wrap their wrists and ankles with bands of colored beads strung to describe geometric patterns and wear gold rings in their noses which are painted along their lengths from brow to tip with black stripes. Most men and women go barefooted.

Women often wear more than half a dozen gold finger rings filed with decorative marks. They are seldom seen without multiple strands of glass beads or heavy necklaces made up of Colombian, Panamanian, or U.S. silver coins. They sometimes wear strings of natural shells, tiny bones, seeds, or gold-plated pendants with attractive patterns etched on them. This regal adornment spectacularly complements the reds and black of mola blouses. Gold earrings of various sizes are worn, but the most dramatic are flat discs sometimes as big as five inches in diameter. A Cuna woman dressed in all her finery presents an exotic and memorable sight.

Because Cunas remained isolated from the world so long and have only recently edged into the mainstream of modern history, their customs and habits have been obscured by a great deal of misinformation. Sometimes it is hard to separate fact from fancy. During all the years they guarded their lands from intrusion they stayed to themselves, did not intermarry, and maintained a strict standard of morals and conduct. Since they made no effort to mingle with outsiders, they were regarded as a mysterious race and legends grew about them. Their neighbors feared them and warned against venturing into their mountain strongholds, but the few intrepid travelers who explored the Cunas' jungle fastness returned safely.

Over the years the Cunas have developed a complicated social system which allows for independence within the

CEREMONIAL CANE

security of the tribe. The major law which governs the group is that no individual should behave in such a way so as to harm his fellow tribesmen. Fred McKim, an American who spent much time with the Cunas in the 1930s, described their government as "a household expanded into a tribe." Modern Cuna life is still rich in customs and steeped in traditions. In fact, there is hardly an occasion from birth to death that is not covered by some rule of behavior. Cunas learn to know all this from the chanted tales and songs that instruct children and grown-ups alike and tell what they should do and how they should act under virtually all circumstances. More important is the tribe's unwritten history which is kept alive by chanting.

Cunas basically believe that all things have souls, that the world is full of good and evil spirits that can help, harm, kill, or cure. These spirits must be avoided, cajoled, tricked, or coaxed, depending on the situation. Such beliefs are the basis for the Cunas' medicine as well as their religion. Witch doctors also have an impressive knowledge of medicinal plants and herbs of the jungle, even medicines to help women become better mola-makers. In addition to chants and herbs, cures are effected by the use of *Uchus*, or carved wooden spirit dolls.

From time to time a whole village will gather at an *Inna* feast to celebrate a young girl's coming of age. The pattern for this celebration, which continues for three days and two nights is predetermined down to the very last gourdful of *chicha*. Guests are expected to drink themselves into a stupor. During the entire ritual the girl is subjected to frequent dousings of cold water in a symbolic cleansing act. The ceremony is culminated by the girl being shorn of her long hair by a woman especially assigned to this task.

Sickness, death, and burial which often travel together

MULTIPLE BRANCH RATTLE

in the islands are also attended by complex rituals.

Cunas believe strongly in an afterlife and conduct themselves accordingly. They are taught that special houses exist in heaven for important members of the community and that one such dwelling is reserved for the best artists. This touching sentiment indicates the importance attributed to mola-making.

The single most important connection between the San Blas Indians and the outside world is the women's mola blouse. These beautifully appliquéd cloth panels are being increasingly exhibited as examples of a unique folk art in major cities throughout the Western world. The mola is a product of acculturation and continues to exist because of tribal tradition. It could never have developed without the cotton cloth, needles, thread, and scissors acquired by trade from the ships that came to barter for coconuts during the 19th century. It is curious to think that the very process of acculturation which has so stimulated mola-making in recent years may also someday destroy it.

Today's life in San Blas continues to change in ways that began nearly forty years ago. Each decade brings the Cuna into closer contact with the outside world, although the elders make efforts to reject some of the more destructive incursions. Acculturation is now a fact, but it is far from breaking down the strong traditional Indian culture that has existed for centuries. In many ways it has enriched Cuna life rather than destroyed it. How long this will remain so is very hard to say. One of the great economic changes in recent years is that the sale of molas has become a major source of income. The simple coconut economy is now a coconut/export labor/mola economy, something that nobody would have dreamed of a decade ago.

Now that the generally negative feelings about outsiders

have softened, small Cuna and foreign-run hotels have opened on a few islands and others are being planned. This tacit encouragement of the tourist trade will bring a deluge of travelers and will help to enrich the islanders who have already had a taste of the other life and can appreciate the things that money will buy. Cunas now go to Panama by the small passenger aircraft that connect the islands to the world, rather then endure the difficult boat trip to Colón. Men going to work in Panama City or the Canal Zone now think in terms of taking their wives and families with them and there is a street in downtown Panama where several Cuna families reside. Although the women still wear their traditional costume in the city, urban life cannot help but change their outlook and eventually affect mola-making.

Rumors of rich mineral deposits on the mainland and a proposed highway along the coast continue to be heard, but so far they have had little effect on San Blas Island life. If the day should come when this adjacent land is opened for exploitation, it will certainly destroy in a few brief years what the Cunas have maintained for centuries. For now these Indians continue to live in harmony with their gods and the flora and fauna of their earth.

ONE-LEGGED UCHU • Uchus *are made as healing aids for specific ailments. This small effigy with the worried expression was probably carved for a man whose leg had been amputated.*

COLOMBIAN TRADER DOCKED AT AILIGANDI • *Colombian trading boats ply the coastal waters of San Blas, visiting the main islands on a regular basis and bringing trade goods to exchange for cash and/or coconuts. Most are sturdy wooden-hulled, two-masted vessels which carry a tantalizing assortment of foods and materials that islanders have learned to depend upon. They spend a few hours or, if business is brisk, several days tied up at the dock and strictly observe a long-standing nonfraternization rule by anchoring at a respectable distance offshore at night. The crew, made up mostly of strapping blacks who tower over the short-statured Cunas, tote huge bags of coconuts to the boat or go among the huts selling household necessities or lengths of colored cloth.*

BALBOA BLOUSE • *The woman who made this delightful blouse copied her design from a convenient Panamanian quarter-of-a-Balboa coin. The breastplate, ruffled collar, and plated shoulder guard adorning the famous explorer's bust have suffered some radical changes due to the Cuna artist's lack of understanding of early Spanish armor. Most striking is Balboa's morion, or crested helmet, which in the Cuna interpretation has exchanged its metallic character for the look of a native campesino's fancy straw-woven hat typical of those worn by Panama's country folk and much like those topping the heads of the quaint figures in the four corners of this mola. The coin's inscription "Un cuarto de Balboa" translates as the equivalent of "one quarter of a dollar."*

MOLAS & THEIR SOURCES

Mola art motifs can be divided into two general but distinct categories: indigenous molas and acculturation molas. The first category includes molas which rely strictly upon traditional designs, both abstract linear patterns and depictions of native flora and fauna, objects from Cuna material culture, and graphically rendered imaginative beings from Cuna myth and legend or pure fantasy creations. Acculturation molas are those inspired by ideas or images from the outside world.

In the beginning when the mola technique was quite new, the San Blas inhabitants decorated their clothing with flora, fauna, and abstract figure designs similar to those traditionally used earlier in body painting. As time went on they began to picture objects from everyday life and, occasionally, impressive things from cultures not their own.

This kind of imagery prevailed without substantial change until the time of WW II when the acculturation process was suddenly accelerated. This change was directly the result of the war. The Panama Canal area needed workmen and hired Cunas who soon found the white man's products much to their liking. From that time on just about anything could and did appear on molas. One of the

PANAMANIAN COIN • *Panama's monetary unit is the Balboa, equal to one United States dollar. The silver coins come in denominations of one Balboa, a half-Balboa, and a quarter, each bearing a likeness of the Spanish conquistador Vasco Núñez de Balboa, whose 1513 adventure has placed him prominently in history books as the first white man to view the Pacific Ocean. A quarter-Balboa piece similar to this one inspired the mola blouse pictured on the opposite page.*

39

RUBBING BASED ON A MAYAN BAS-RELIEF
•This large rubbing portrays El Hechicero, the shamanistic Enchanter, or Witch Doctor, wearing an elegant headdress, robed in a leopard's skin, face painted chalky white, and performing a curative ritual by blowing smoke through a reed pipe. Cuna medicine men also perform smoke-blowing rituals so it is not surprising that, once encountered, this same figure would appear on a modern mola. It is based on a bas-relief temple carving from the Mayan ruins of Palenque in Mexico.

AZTEC AND MAYAN FIGURES • *Exotic pre-Columbian art holds as much fascination for Cuna mola-makers as it does for archaeologists and art lovers. This panel brings together an Aztec warrior god and a Mayan witch doctor in a set piece reminiscent of ancient codices or early Aztec picture books. The smaller figure on the right is a crude copy of a very sophisticated carving from the classical period of Mayan art. This naïve Cuna interpretation hardly compares to the original but the form is unmistakable.*

VARIATIONS ON A PRE-HISPANIC DESIGN
• *The three illustrations seen on this page dramatically trace an artistic metamorphosis from an ancient pottery motif to a modern-day mola. The original is a wonderfully stylized little figure, thought by some to be a Turtle God, painted on an early polychrome plate discovered at the Sitio Conte archaeological site in the province of Coclé. The second shows the same archaic design neatly trimmed down for use as a symbol for the Panamanian national television channel. And, twice removed but still drawing upon Panama's rich pre-Hispanic heritage, the third illustration shows a Cuna artist's interpretation of the same figure now employed as a mola design, freer in form and glowing with its own naïve charm.*

MOLA BASED ON TV SYMBOL

LION MOLA FROM PRINTED CLOTH SOURCE • *The search for mola design sources is a fascinating if often frustrating and misleading endeavor. On the San Blas island of Rio Sidra in 1973 this storybook lion appeared on several blouses before a happy coincidence brought source and stitched design together* on the same garment. *The yoke, made of printed fabric, supplied the rather childish image which a Cuna woman's artistry and expert needlework developed into this delightfully gentled King of Beasts.*

few taboos is the subject of sex, for, unlike many primitive societies, Cunas are reserved about such matters and sexual images are rarely if ever found on molas.

Acculturation molas could be considered the great contemporary copy art. When the designs are looked at side by side with their sources, the magic of Cuna interpretation can be appreciated. Unpleasing details are eliminated and something new is always added to support or enhance the design, and shapes are shortened, widened, repeated, patterned, and embellished in dozens of different ways.

FISHNET TWINE LABEL

FISH NET TWINE LABEL • *The circular device in this mola is not an Origin of Life symbol but the center part of a label design from a spool of Roseland Seine Twine, exported by the Grady-Travers Company based in New York. This became a very popular motif in the 1950s but has fallen from fashion in recent years, along with the all cotton product it represented which has now been replaced by nylon. The mola's source, pictured here, is a handsome "La Rosita" brand label showing three fish encircling a rose. The design must have held a great attraction for mola-makers for it showed up in numerous variations over the years, more often than not with lettering scrambled beyond recognition.*

MOLA FROM FISHNET TWINE LABEL   43

SHOTGUN-SHELLS BOX • *On hunting trips to the mainland Cuna men use 12- and 16-gauge shotguns to bring down large game like deer and wild pigs and .22 caliber rifles for birds and smaller game. Shotgun shells are expensive but necessary for jungle hunting, and Western's Super X brand seems to be a popular choice.*

SUPER X MOLA • *One woman was intrigued by the bold Super X logo on the side of her husband's box of shotgun shells. When she began a new mola she used it as her basic design, embellishing it with tiny flowers and a varicolored background.*

CUNA RATTLES • *Cunas use rattles to make rhythmic sounds and to mark time for ceremonial chants and dances. Mothers shake them soothingly as they sing lullabies and gently swing their babies to sleep in hammocks. This mola-maker used several gourd rattles to decorate her brightly colored blouse, arranging them in a pleasant, size-graduated pattern, and enhancing them with rich appliqué.*

GOURD RATTLES IN BASKET • *Rattles, usually made from gourds filled with dried seeds or pebbles, are a common household object. Some are beautifully incised with geometric patterns and have cord wrapped wooden sticks for handles. When shaken in a certain way they produce a rasping but distinctly musical sound.*

HOW MOLAS ARE MADE & HOW TO JUDGE THEM

DETAIL OF TURTLE FORMS

Molas, the pictorial blouses worn by Cuna Indian women in Panama's San Blas Islands, are made from panels of two or more layers of cloth cut and tucked under to reveal the colors beneath. The technique is usually called appliqué, though referred to occasionally as reverse appliqué. Sometimes embellishments of embroidery or rickrack are also used. The process requires previsualization and ingenuity. Cuna girls are continuously exposed to mola-making from birth; they begin to sew practice molas at about age seven and develop virtuosity by the time they reach marriageable age. The basic technique of making a mola is described in the caption on page 49.

DETAILS OF APPLIQUÉ TECHNIQUES • *Undecorated color areas are not tolerated on good molas. Spaces are cleverly broken up in various ways. Tiny circles are cut out of the background to reveal a different color underneath (upper left) making an overall texture. The most commonly used method is to make vertical cuts which are then tucked and sewn. These can be delicate or clumsy, depending on the mola's quality (upper right). A method which is becoming increasingly popular is to snip triangular shapes out of the background and then replace them with different-colored smaller triangles one or two layers thick (lower left). A less frequently used way of breaking up space is seen on the rooster's feathers at lower right where oddly shaped pieces of cloth are added in an almost sculptural manner.*

DETAIL SHOWING APPLIQUÉD CIRCLES

DETAIL SHOWING APPLIQUÉD VERTICAL CUTS

DETAIL SHOWING APPLIQUÉD TRIANGLES

DETAIL SHOWING ODD-PIECE APPLIQUÉ

47

Molas are best viewed from a distance of at least six feet in order to see color relationships and make sense of the design elements. Regardless of content, whether the mola depicts a simple bird form, an abstract pattern, or a vignette of Cuna village life, its ultimate success must depend on the artist's ability to capture the essence of her chosen subject. If she fails, no amount of careful cutting and sewing can elevate that work to more than a fine piece of stitchery. However, there are molas, particularly older ones, in which the technique is comparatively crude, but the graphic statement is so strong that lack of perfection does not detract. Another important consideration of quality is the care with which a mola is made. In fine work the outline layers should be even, corners should be graceful and not lumpy, stitches should be tiny, even hidden. Economy of line is no virtue. When a mola is scrutinized, there should be no areas in the design that seem neglected.

Most molas show a degree of fading unless they are panels made strictly for the tourist trade and have never been worn as part of a blouse. Fading is a normal consequence of a mola's workaday life, an echo of frequent washings and months or years of hard wear in the fierce tropical sun. It is usually more pronounced on the upper part of a panel because blouses are worn tucked into wraparound skirts. Faded molas should be judged individually and with perspicacity by collectors. Many otherwise beautiful molas show signs of hard usage, but mending, backing, and careful framing can salvage such forlorn pieces and preserve them for the works of art they are.

Design copying from other molas or outside sources is an integral, healthy, and indispensable aspect of mola-making. In fact, although occasional designs are so complex or difficult that they defy imitation, a major test of the

HALF-FINISHED MOLA • *Several basic mola-making techniques can be understood from the construction of this comparatively simple unfinished work. The front panel (illustrated) and back panel (not illustrated) each started with three cotton rectangles. On the front panel the bottom layer is red and, typically, of a heavier, more textured cotton than subsequent layers. The middle layer is orange, and the top layer is black (as seen in the folded back lower left corner). On the reverse side the bottom layer is of the same coarse red cloth, the middle is yellow, and the top a darker red. The three dominant figures are cut out of the middle and top layers of both panels and switched to the same position on the reverse panel (actually done in two steps but considered as one here to simplify the principle). This switching explains why the fronts and backs of most contemporary molas have the same design but with major color areas reversed, a simple matter of economy rather than aesthetics.*

Look next at the vertical cutaway slits of the black background. With the exception of orange (the middle layer), the colors showing through come from small pieces of colored cloth inserted under the top layer (pink in the lower left corner). This addition of small swatches explains the variety of colors seen in most present-day molas.

Consider next each bottle shape, made up of two additional layers placed on top of the three basic layers. The unfinished bottles in the upper left show how the multicolored underlayers are cut, tucked, and stitched before adding the black (pinned back). Note how, on the larger bottle shapes, scraps of cloth are again inserted.

To finish the mola, several more vertical slits will be added, faces and drinking straws will be completed, the green nose will become black outlined in green, white teeth and eyes will appear, and faces will be textured with stitchery.

Page 220 shows the source for this design alongside an earlier, more finely worked interpretation.

In applying this description to other molas, think of a middle point in the cloth layers. Some effects are achieved by cutting away from this point to reveal underlayers, whereas others come from building up additional layers which may then also be cut away in some areas.

appeal of a newly introduced image is how soon and how widely it is cribbed.

This book deals with molas as folk art. Not included are most mola panels made for tourists, *molitas*, mola patches, fashionable clothing, handbags, toys, and other objects decorated with Cuna appliqué. The quality of workmanship on these tourist products varies from good to indifferent, and they are not true mola art.

BACK OF ABSTRACT FAUNA DESIGN WITH CROSSES • *Quite often a mola will reveal its fine craftsmanship if studied from the back. The tiny, evenly spaced stitches of the small turtle lodged in the belly of the larger one pictured below show up clearly against their black underlayer, whereas on the front they are intentionally hidden by clever needlework.*

ABSTRACT FAUNA DESIGN WITH CROSSES • *When reducing flowers or animals to a semiabstract pattern Cunas seem to have an uncanny feel for balance and design. Usually no more than two or three colors are used in molas of this type, although occasionally a touch of some unexpected hue is added for dramatic effect. Some collectors believe a good mola has to have several layers of cloth but this is not necessarily true. Abstract and geometric molas can be exquisite in design and workmanship using only two or three layers.*

MYTHICAL CREATURES • *This needlecrafted mélange of mythical creatures, although somewhat sun-bleached in its upper area, is an excellent blending of fine stitchery and intriguing subject matter. Represented are three Eastern deities—Garuda, in cosmic flight; the demon, Pazuzu, Father of the Winds; and the Hindu god, Vishnu, holding a lotus blossom, in one of his many guises. Commercially dyed cotton mola cloth withstands much wear and frequent washing as well as exposure to the harsh tropical sun, but many of the older blouses do, however, show signs of wear and fading. This does not necessarily mean a beautifully worked mola should be rejected by discerning collectors. Sometimes fading mutes the garish colors and strangely enhances their beauty, lending an aura of baraka, a hint of personal history.*

BACK OF ABSTRACT FAUNA DESIGN
WITH CROSSES

MYTHICAL CREATURES

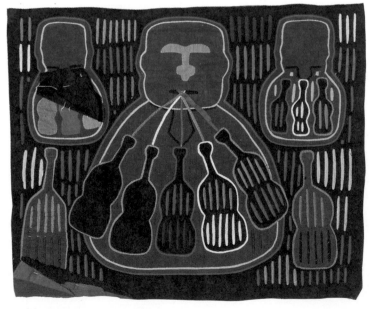

ABSTRACT FAUNA DESIGN WITH CROSSES

HALF-FINISHED MOLA

BIRD AND SERPENT • *Hard and fast rules can prove delusive when trying to judge the merits of molas. There are, however, certain elements which most fine molas have in common, some of which can be clearly studied in this intricate pattern. Primarily there is the comprehensive artistic concept, the confrontation between bird and serpent, set in a multitude of plant forms. The design is exciting, well balanced, and dynamic. The craftsmanship is readily apparent in the artist's skillful tucking and layering of cloth as well as in her precise* stitchery. *The patterning is evenly distributed, leaving no weak or empty areas, and the colors are carefully chosen, recurring several times within the design. When compared point by point with the half-finished example on the preceding page, it is easy to see that this masterful creation was made by a more talented and dedicated mola-maker. It is unusual to find a signed mola, but this artist, Beatriz Martinez, was evidently pleased enough with her handiwork to stitch her name across the bird's body for all to see.*

51

HISTORIC, ABSTRACT, & GEOMETRIC DESIGNS

OLD MOLA WITH TRADITIONAL PAT-
TERN • *What the Cunas call* mola seret, *or old mola, still turns up occasionally. This one was found in the late 1960s on one of the remoter islands. Judging from its coarse cloth and faded and worn condition, one could say it dated from the 1920s or early 1930s. Though seldom used on contemporary molas this design was once most fashionable.*

The mola blouse came into being a little over 100 years ago. Its design origins were a natural extension of body painting which the Cunas had practiced for centuries.

Lionel Wafer described this custom in 1699: "They make figures of birds, beasts, men, trees, or the like . . . but the figures are not extraordinary like what they represent, and are of differing dimensions, as their fancies lead them. The women are the painters, and take great delight in it. The colors they like to use most are red, yellow and blue, very bright and lovely." Slightly altered, this observation could be aptly used to describe mola art.

After migrating from mainland villages, Cunas on the San Blas Islands came into frequent contact with Yankee sailing ships whose crews bartered goods for coconuts. Although some cloth had been traded since the 1700s, new encounters introduced the essential material ingredients—commercial cloth, thread, needles, thimbles, and scissors—without which molas would never have developed.

The connecting link between body painting and the crude first attempts at appliqué may well have been the

OLD WOMAN WEARING "GRAND-MOTHER MOLA" • *Many of the older Cuna women wear molas styled after those that were typical of their younger years. These are called Mukan or "grandmother molas" distinguished by their ample size and choice of traditional or comparatively simple designs. Even today, when making new blouses, these women more often than not go back to their favorite patterns of earlier times. Nor do they push to sell their needlework, tending rather to stay somewhat aloof from negotiations with tourists. Also, in keeping with an earlier time, they wear the larger and narrower gold nose rings.*

LEGENDS FOR FOLLOWING PAGES:

EARLY MOLAS FROM THE BRITISH MUSEUM COLLECTION • *The illustrations on the two pages that follow are typical of mola design and construction during the first two decades of the twentieth century. These blouses were collected by an adventurous English woman, Lady Richmond Brown, and her fellow countryman, F. A. Mitchell Hedges, during an unusual trip to both island and mainland Cuna villages in 1922. Part of their vast collection of over sixteen hundred pieces of "hieroglyphic cloth," one hundred carvings, and nearly a thousand necklaces was given to the British Museum. Distinct differences can be noted between these and contemporary molas. Blouses of this period were made of coarser cloth and had larger appliquéd panels with fitted yokes and sleeves. Printed fabric was used more frequently in the panels and less so in the yoke-sleeve area, quite the opposite from today's styles. While the majority of these early blouses show plant and animal forms, geometric, abstract, and repeat patterns, there are also molas depicting anchors with chains, parasols, and sailing vessels that show the beginning effects of acculturation.*

EARLY MOLA: SERPENT MOTIF

EARLY MOLA: REPEAT PATTERN

EARLY MOLA: NUMEROUS SHIPS

EARLY MOLA: ABSTRACT DESIGN

EARLY MOLA: FOUR ANIMALS

EARLY MOLA: ABSTRACT GEOMETRIC DESIGN

EARLY MOLA: TWO ANIMALS

EARLY MOLA: ABSTRACT FLORAL PATTERN

55

THREE ABSTRACT MOTIFS • *Although at first glance abstract designs may appear technically less complicated than pictorial molas, they often entail weeks of painstaking labor. In the example at top right the artist has introduced over four hundred crenulations, each of which had to be carefully cut and tucked in before sewing. Below are two other designs whose apparent simplicity is deceiving, especially the one on the left, which describes a maze of saw-toothed lines. These are a far cry from what are called "tourist molas" made expressly for export and sale to day-trippers who visit the islands with tours. As soon as a woman begins making molas for an outside market rather than for her own use, a devastating change of attitude takes place and time inevitably becomes equated with money. Unfortunately most tourist encounters lead Cunas to believe that the easy market is in simple, gaudy mola panels that are quickly produced and carelessly stitched. It is a sad replay of an oft-repeated twentieth-century drama—the corruption and/or death of a contemporary folk art at the hands of an undiscriminating public.*

CRENULATED PATTERN

56   SAW-TOOTHED MAZE   SEEDPOD MOTIF

decorated cotton undergarments worn by Cuna women in the late 1800s. It is not clear whether the bright colors of former times had been abandoned but black and indigo blue came into vogue, the pigments being applied with chewed stick brushes. Designs were mostly geometric repeat patterns similar to both body painting motifs and those soon to follow on molas.

Clothing must have been an outside innovation as well as an imposition on these tropical Indians—a supposition which lends credence to the theory that missionary zeal was at least partly responsible for its introduction.

In Victorian times Cuna men were already wearing shirts and trousers, and the women dressed in loose-fitting, light-colored or indigo-blue chemises. Sometime toward the mid-19th century it became fashionable, if not outright defiant, to attach a bright red band to the hem of this otherwise plain garment.

As a greater variety of colored cloth became available, it was only a matter of time before some ingenious soul cut pieces of cloth in the form of traditionally familiar designs. These beginnings were humble but critical. The bands became decorated with simple appliqué as experimentation continued. Tribal societies are imitative by nature; soon most women were involved with this new idea. As the practice caught on, the decorative band gradually widened until it covered most of the front and back areas of the garment, which was, in the meantime, becoming shorter.

Thus the mola blouse was born and by the turn of the 20th century it was on its way to becoming a thriving textile art.

LEGENDS FOR FOLLOWING PAGE:

ABSTRACT AND GEOMETRIC PATTERNS
• *Although mola-making during the past quarter century has leaned more and more toward pictorial and acculturation themes, exceptional work is still being done with abstract and geometric designs. Some women seem to prefer the traditional patterns, whereas others turn to them only on occasion. When younger artists do attempt this type of mola, the results are often technically superior to similar examples from the past. Just as mola-makers have become more competitive so have sewing techniques improved. Overall design has become tighter and the dramatic use of color more effectively controlled. The best artists seem absolutely in control of their medium and can make it do whatever they please. Color vibrations have become more intense in recent years and are designed to achieve the maximum optical effect. Indeed, Cuna mola-makers seem to do intuitively what many modern-day artists consciously strive for in Pop and Op Art.*

The four distinctly different designs pictured on the next page represent the broad, rich range of contemporary nonpictorial molas. Some collectors are especially drawn to these abstract and geometric motifs because they believe that pure design or non-representational patterns are the only true molas. Others collect only molas that tell a story, while still others seek only designs that can be verified as strictly the result of acculturation.

Whether it be pure design, story molas, or acculturation molas, there are, fortunately, enough to go around. Molas are made in the tens of thousands every year. The workmanship gets better, and there is certainly no dearth of ideas for new designs, even those that elaborate upon traditional abstract and geometric patterns.

ABSTRACT FLORAL DESIGN

ABSTRACT FLORAL DESIGN

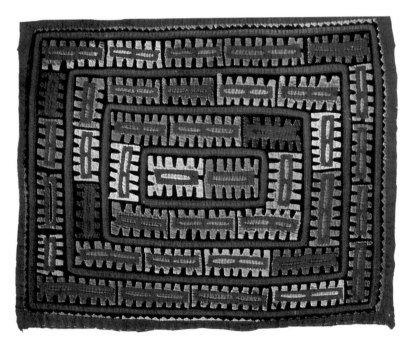

GEOMETRIC REPEAT PATTERN

GEOMETRIC REPEAT PATTERN

ABSTRACT FAUNA DESIGN • *When creating abstract patterns, especially complex ones, Cuna artists often turn to color combinations which they would not ordinarily use in pictorial molas. Colors are deliberately put together to set up visual vibrations that tantalize and trick the eye. In such designs, not only choice of colors but also complexity and weight of line must be carefully considered in order to achieve the desired effect.*

59

SCENES OF EVERYDAY CUNA LIFE

One of the most appealing aspects of life in the San Blas Islands is a kind of primordial rhythm which flows through the whole society. The structured day begins early in Cuna villages and follows a simple but meaningful routine. The soft sounds of people stirring are heard long before daybreak, the creak of hammock ropes, the thump of bare feet against earthen floors, the swish of reed fans as logs are shoved into fire pits and sleeping embers are fanned into flame. Cooking utensils clatter as the early morning drink is prepared from plantains and sugarcane juice. Tiny kerosene lamps light the darkened huts as flickering shadows chase each other across bamboo walls.

Voices are kept to a whisper, but somewhere the incongruous crackle of a transistor radio can be heard blaring out agricultural reports in rapid Spanish, interspersed with bursts of Latin-American music from Radio Havana

MOLA PATCH • *In the past several years literally thousands of small appliquéd pieces called* pachis, *or "mola patches" have been made in San Blas, particularly on the islands most frequently visited by tourists. This new phenomenon stemmed directly from the youthful craze in the United States and elsewhere for sewing decorative patches onto denim clothing, and Cunas quickly realized that they had another highly salable product. Though often charming, these patches are made strictly for the tourist trade and have little to do with true mola-making.*

MOLA-MAKER SEWING IN HAMMOCK • *A Cuna woman's sewing basket is seldom far from her side. Between chores she industriously stitches on one of the several molas she may have in progress at the same time. This mother whiles away a warm afternoon outside her hut, relaxing in a hammock and swinging her sleepy child gently back and forth as she sews on a mola planned for wear at the island's next* chicha *festival. She has laid aside the figured, red cotton head scarf used to cover her cropped hair, as do the women in their own homes, and concentrates solely upon her sewing, oblivious to the world about her.*

LEGENDS FOR FOLLOWING PAGE:

YOUNG WOMAN PAINTING NOSE STRIPE
• *Most women and female children regularly paint a vertical black line down the center of their noses using a dye made from the juice of the* Saptur *tree (Genipa americana), the Cuna's Sacred Tree of Life. Practiced mainly as a beauty custom nowadays, there are still remnants of a strong belief that this magical line keeps away evil.*

CUNA MOTHER SEWING MOLA • *One of the more commonplace scenes in any San Blas village is that of a Cuna mother sewing a mola as she swings her infant child to sleep in a hammock. Dressed in all her finery, including colorfully beaded arm and leg bands, golden nose ring, necklace, and earrings, she is depicted here surrounded by other members of her family inside their bamboo hut. Also shown are her sewing basket and nippled baby's bottle, indicating that she has begun to accept modern ways.*

HULLING AND WINNOWING RICE
• *A man and woman are hulling rice in the traditional manner, using large wooden mortar and pestles. The smaller figures seated beneath the man are winnowing the grain.*

CAYUCO TRIP • *Travel from island to island or to the mainland is part of the Cuna's daily routine. Here a* cayuco *is shown rigged for sail. Two men with paddles are transporting a woman passenger to her destination.*

61

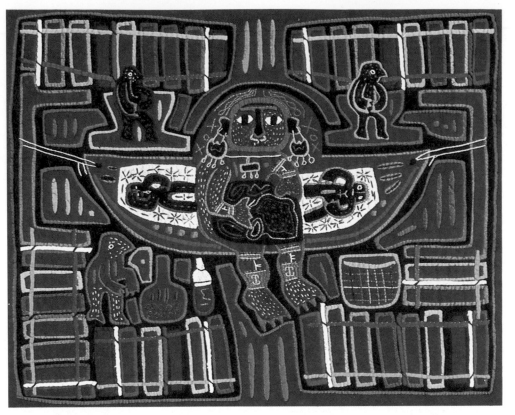

YOUNG WOMAN PAINTING NOSE STRIPE   CUNA MOTHER SEWING MOLA

HULLING AND WINNOWING RICE   CAYUCA TRIP

CUNA COUNCIL MEETING • *This is an exploded view from above of the lantern-lit interior of a council house with a typical meeting in session. At these nightly gatherings the men usually keep their hats on, and some men carry ceremonial canes. Also included are women, some with babies, who sit opposite their men. Here an orator is addressing two saylas, or headmen, who lounge in hammocks, one smoking a pipe as he swings and judiciously listens. Spectators wander in and out during these lengthy meetings, and in this mola one has stretched out on a bench and is taking a nap.*

OLD WOMAN SMOKING PIPE

CUNA FIRE FAN

FIRE FAN MOLA

FIRE TENDING • *Fires are kept going constantly in Cuna huts and fire fans are essential items to every household. Slow-burning logs are placed in a star formation flat on the earthen floor and when heat for cooking is needed their smoldering ends are shoved together and fanned briskly into flame. Tending the fire is a respectable position usually entrusted to old women. The pipe-smoking matriarch in this photograph can be depended upon to be out of her hammock and have a breakfast fire going long before each day's dawn. The decorative, reed-woven fan below is one of a pair used for breathing new life into glowing embers. The mola, with its familiar motif, depicts a common San Blas scene—an old woman sitting on a crude wooden stool as she smokes her pipe and tends the fire with grandly exaggerated fans.*

64

or Panama City and rock 'n' roll from the U.S. station in the Canal Zone. Occasionally the unmusical voice of a witch doctor effecting a cure or an old man practicing ceremonial chants can be heard for hours on end.

There is always the barely audible activity of men leaving for the mainland, their soft voices calling out as preparations are made, the women helping to load the dugouts, the dull wooden clatter of paddles, axes, and hoes, sail and mast being loaded aboard, and finally the heaving together as the heavy boat is shoved over short log rollers into the sea with a splash.

As day breaks, a fleet of *cayucos* loaded with empty calabashes can be seen headed for the mainland as women paddle over to bring back the day's fresh supply of river water. The men whose turn it is to work the garden plots have long since departed.

By late morning the men have returned from their jungle plantations. Boats are unloaded and food is prepared. The midday meal consists of heaping portions of boiled rice or yucca with plantain and chunks or fish or, occasionally, wild game stirred in. There is also coffee or a hot drink made of mashed plantain sweetened with cane juice. And, when in season, an abundance of fresh fruit—bananas, mangoes, mamey, oranges. Meals are not imaginative, although there is variety with fish, tiny crabs, lobsters, chicken, and iguana meat to relieve the starchy diet.

A long *siesta* is observed during afternoons when the sun is hottest. The village becomes quiet and people rest. Later, children play games or amuse themselves swimming. Teen-agers play basketball and a few study schoolbook lessons. The men weave baskets, work with their boats, or go off to other islands on missions of one kind or another. Sometimes they spend hours just playing with

LEGENDS FOR FOLLOWING PAGE:

FRUIT GATHERING • *In their season tropical fruits can be plentiful in the Darien jungle. They come in great variety and help to supplement the starchy diet which is usually the Cunas' daily fare. Fruit gathering is a family affair; they paddle to the mainland, seek out a prosperous tree, attack its branches with sticks, and fill their baskets. It is not certain whether the center figure is simply a member of the harvest team or is intended, as some interpreters say, to represent the spirit of the forest tree.*

HUNTERS • *When Cunas go to the mainland to tend their garden plots they often shoot wild game for the cooking pot. Pictured here are two agile hunters climbing palm trees in order to spot their quarry, which, in this case, may be the simian-looking figure on the left.*

INDIANS WITH IGUANAS • *Just as the sea around San Blas teems with marine life so does the jungle abound in exotic fauna. This mola is a whimsical collage of man, bird, beast, and reptile. It shows two boys, waist deep in water, holding aloft freshly caught starfish; two women carrying wild animals of some sort in their arms; and two men bringing home three very large iguanas destined for the cooking pot.*

65

DETAIL FROM HUNTERS

FRUIT GATHERING

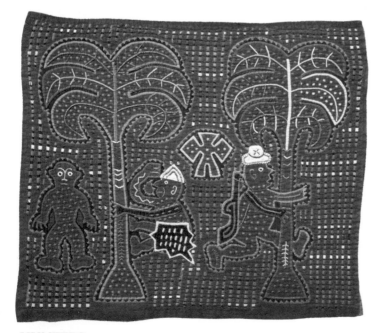

66

HUNTERS

INDIANS WITH IGUANAS

ISLAND ACTIVITIES • *The simple life in San Blas provides the inhabitants with a variety of daily activities. In this complex mola men are portrayed sailing and paddling their cayucos, gathering coconuts, playing the guitar, and resting in the shade of a tropical tree.*

WASHBOARDS, OLD AND NEW

WOMEN USING WASHBOARDS

WASHBOARDS • *Even the most mundane chores are sometimes recreated on molas. When Cuna women paddle to the mainland for fresh water they also bathe and do their family's laundry. San Blas Indians are noted for their cleanliness, but the laundry routine is also a social activity. The photograph emphasizes the effects of acculturation by showing a hand-carved, old-style wooden washboard alongside a modern one. On the upper mola two women are using washboards identified in Spanish as rayo while on the one below the job is done, the clothes, neatly labeled, are hung on a line to dry, and the scented soap, Jabon Lux, is put to rest on the board's wooden ledge.*

68

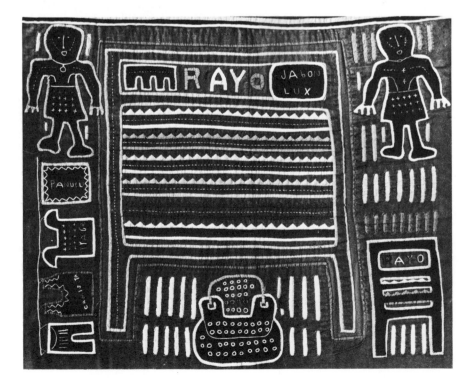

THE LAUNDRY

their youngsters, whom they seem to adore. The women and girls sit on log benches in front of their huts chatting and sewing on molas. Others work in the cool indoors.

There is always a flurry of activity when the big trading boats come in. Coconuts are counted, sold, and loaded from individual and community stores. Commodities are purchased as both men and women gather to make deals. The Colombians, mostly tall husky blacks, carry huge loads of coconuts to the boats; some of the more enterprising roam the village with bolts of colored cloth, selling lengths of it from door to door. The boats stay docked for several hours, then move on to other islands. If they remain until dark, they anchor some distance offshore so that they do not violate Cuna hospitality or an unwritten law, now somewhat relaxed, that forbade strangers from staying overnight.

The whole community turns out to celebrate a girl's coming of age. There is feasting, dancing to the accompaniment of reed flutes and pipes of Pan, a very formalized foot-stamping, quick turning dance with men lined up on one side and women on the other. There is much ceremonial smoking and drinking. The men gather inside the big hut where *chicha* is served from gourds dipped into large special clay jars. They talk, laugh, blow smoke into one another's faces, and get very drunk. If they pass out, they are carried to hammocks in the *chicha* hut or are taken home to sober up before rejoining the feast. The *Inna* feast lasts three days and on the last day the women drink and are soon in a state of stupor too. Dressed in all their finery—gold necklaces, gorgeous pendants, and saucer-sized earring discs—the women use this occasion to show off their newest and best molas.

Meetings are held nightly in the council lodge set aside

LEGENDS FOR FOLLOWING PAGE:

CATCHING A MANTA RAY • *Manta rays, or devil fish, frequent the waters of San Blas and are sometimes caught by Cuna fishermen. Because of the great size and ferocity of the fish, a dozen men may be required to land one. This graphic study, dated 1962, commemorates one such epic struggle. The boatmen have harpooned their quarry and the battle is about to begin. Fortunately, there are enough aids standing by to haul it ashore should the situation get out of hand.*

CUTTING UP A WHALE • *This huge denizen of the deep looks like a whale although it is labeled a* caballo del mar, *or sea horse, rather than the Spanish* ballena. *It appears to have been brought to shore by a single boat, no mean feat in itself. While the harpoons are being removed an army of men and boys have set about cutting it up with flensing tools resembling exaggerated hatchets and knives. It is interesting to note that old-time ships' logs show that Cuna men (who still go to sea as merchant seamen) frequently sailed aboard U. S. whaling vessels in the 19th century.*

INTERISLAND BOAT AT DOCK • *Some of the more enterprising Indians have acquired their own fair-sized motor-powered boats and conduct a profitable cargo and passenger service among the islands and to Colón, the major Panamanian city on the Atlantic coast. Here is the Cuna boat,* San Ignacio of Tupile, *anchored and tying up at the landing dock of a San Blas island village. The pilot stays at his helm as sailors maneuver the craft close to dock with mooring lines. One passenger, bag in hand, seems ready to disembark, and others remain seated beneath the sailcloth canopy that protects them from the scorching sun. Along with a native hut is one of the islands' few two-storey concrete-block structures, either a schoolhouse or a trading center.*

DETAIL FROM CATCHING
A MANTA RAY

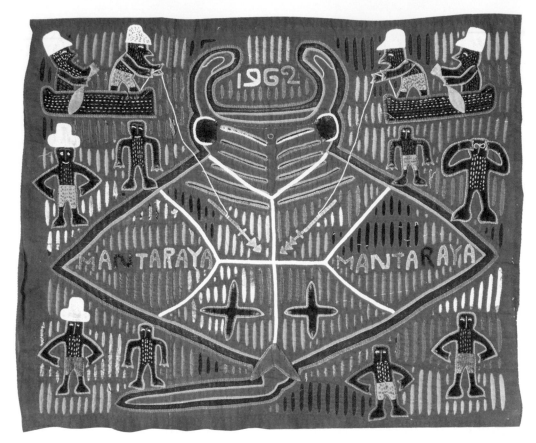

CATCHING A MANTA RAY

CUTTING UP A WHALE

INTERISLAND BOAT AT DOCK

70

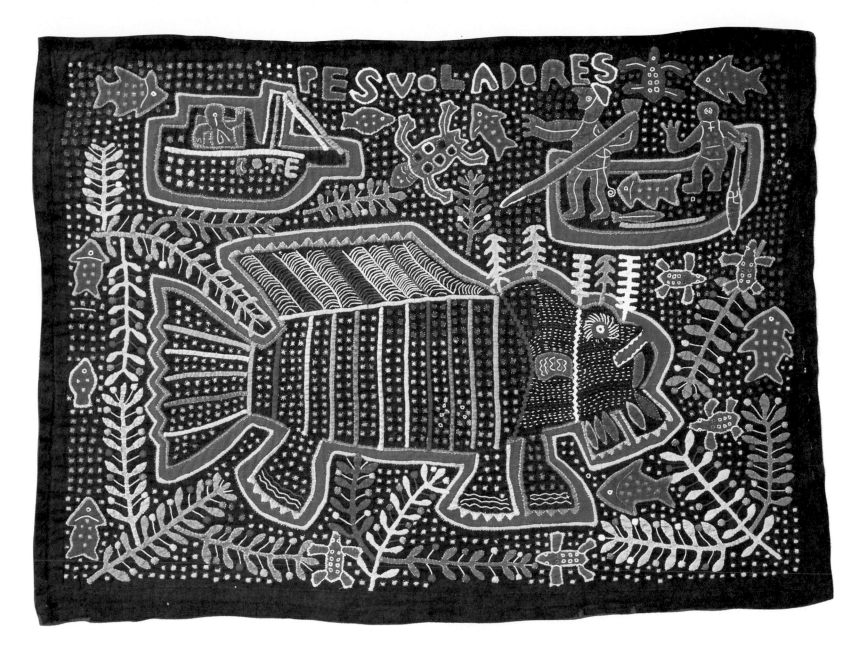

FLYING FISH • *This Cuna interpretation of* pes voladores, *or flying fish,
is a masterpiece of imaginative needlecraft. Besides its naïvely rendered
figures—the grotesque flying fish, the seven turtles, lacy strands of seaweed,
and diverse forms of fishes—there are hundreds of tiny decorative dots, each
snipped out and painstakingly stitched, representing untold hours of eyestrain
and nimble thimble work. The two boats are carefully differentiated; the* bote
is plainly a motor launch, while the other is a cayuco *with two men aboard,
one wielding a harpoon, his companion a paddle.*

SICKNESS

DEATH

SICKNESS • *Sickness and death among Cunas are accompanied with a great deal of ritual rarely seen by outsiders. The images on this page are a pair, front and back of the same blouse, and record in sequence two related events. The first scene shows the interior of a hut where a sick man has taken to his hammock and is being ministered to by a medicine man while his wife and child look on. The medicine man, seated on a stool and holding a ritualistic cane topped by a carved and painted bird, is reciting the healing incantations. Hot pepper incense burns in the clay pot beneath his hammock, and spirits in the form of birds hover aloft, as though seeking to escape the smoke-filled dwelling.*

DEATH • *In the second panel we must assume that the witch doctor's cure did not work and that his ailing patient has died. The dead man has been wrapped in his hammock and is being carried off for burial accompanied by family members and a fluttering bird (bearing a striking resemblance to the features of the deceased) that follows along and is intended to represent his soul. The dead man's belongings, gifts, and food for the long journey to the other world are strung on a line above him. An attitude of sadness affects the procession, and even the trees have assumed postures of grief.*

CUNA WAKE • *Death in San Blas is attended by strict mourning rituals. This mola depicts a scene that is rarely portrayed on blouses—a Cuna wake. The deceased is shown lying serenely in his hammock ministered to by the* massartule, *or death chanter, who, with his symbolic cane, will sing death chants continually for twenty-four hours. At the far side of the room six female mourners sit resignedly with arms folded and their heads properly covered. Incense pots containing sweet-smelling cocoa beans are placed under the hammock, and the two men at the left have stuck a row of sacred sticks into the earth to help protect the deceased.*

CUNA BURIAL • *Sometimes a mola accurately reveals an aspect of Cuna culture otherwise rarely seen by outsiders. The artist who made this commemorative mola depicts in detail the burial customs of San Blas. Shown here is a cutaway diagram of a typical Cuna grave. The hammock in which the body is wrapped is suspended from two vertical* posts. A soulboat, containers of food for the long and perilous journey to the afterlife, and the dead man's possessions (including two kerosene lamps) are placed on the floor of the tomb. A roof is constructed by short logs laid side by side over the burial pit. Articles of the deceased's clothing (not shown here) are spread over the logs and *suelo*, or the excavated earth, is piled on to form a gentle mound. On top of this mound a low table is spread with more containers of food. Two stools for mourners and what appears to be a pair of wreaths (a Christian innovation) are also shown. The topmost lettering, spanning the distance between two ominous-looking spirit figures, indicates that the grave is occupied by a *kantule*, or chanter, named Oscar, who died in 1960. It is further stated below that he was a "mask champion," probably a maker of ceremonial masks.

CUNA WAKE

CUNA BURIAL

HOT PEPPER INCENSE MAN • *This revealing mola depicts a local medicine man making a hut call carrying pots of green pepper incense, the fumes of which are supposed to ward off devils and evil spirits, all of whom detest smoke, the hot pepper variety most of all. The incense is lighted by hot coals and the pots are placed under the hammocks of sick people or around anyone who might be in danger of having his soul snatched away by devils.*

for government and community functions. These are presided over by two or three *saylas*, head chiefs of the island, who recline in hammocks as they judiciously listen to disputes or simply discuss the day's happenings. Whatever thorny problems arise among the villagers are settled there, the word of the headmen being final. Meetings are informal and people wander in and out as they please.

School is not compulsory so only about half the children attend. By the age of ten or twelve, boys are regularly accompanying their fathers to the mainland learning to tend crops and gather food and firewood. Girls help with the cooking, go to collect fresh water, and practice sewing under their mothers' supervision. One can walk through a Cuna village at night and see inside many huts where women, old and young, sit clustered in the yellow glow of a kerosene lamp as they sew on molas.

Funerals are highly ritualistic. Women wail and chanters sing dirges. Incense is burned to keep away evil spirits and there is a tobacco smoke ceremony shared by the mourners. Interment takes place on the mainland in community burial sites located in great open-sided longhouses with thatched roofs. Graves are dug into hard clay, and the dead person is wrapped in a hammock and suspended in the burial pit, which is then covered over to form a mound. A few belongings and food for the journey to the other world are also added.

Nearly all of these scenes from daily life have, at one time or another, appeared on mola blouses. Such appliquéd panels are as remarkable for their pictorial content as they are for their brilliant colors and fine stitchery. Their detailed vignettes of village activities provide unerring insights into Cuna life and culture.

LEGENDS FOR FOLLOWING PAGE:

CHICHA-MAKING • *The four molas on the next page all have to do with one very important aspect of Cuna life, the ceremonial feast, in which the whole community generally participates.* Chicha, *a potent drink made from sugarcane juice mixed with herbs and corn, is consumed in great quantities at all important festivals. In this carefully stitched mola, pipe-smoking women stir the brew in huge cauldrons as their men solemnly fan the log fires. The ladles are used to transfer the boiled liquid into wide-mouthed jars where it will ferment in about two weeks.*

CEREMONIAL DANCING • *There are many occasions for ceremonial dances on the San Blas Islands. Traditionally the women shake rattles and stamp bare-footed rhythms while the men play reed pipes of Pan. The artist who created this mola must have had in mind a recent festivity because she specifically named the dancers who were, no doubt, her friends. She also humorously labeled it the "Cha-cha-cha of Nookope."*

FESTIVAL MUSICIANS • *Two* kantules, *or high priests, in modern neckties and traditional feathered headdresses, accompanied by their assistants, play reed flutes at a young girl's puberty celebration.*

INEBRIATION AT AN INNA FEAST • *Although alcoholic consumption in everyday life is frowned upon by Cunas, ritualistic drunkenness plays an important part in tribal ceremonies. After imbibing too much* chicha *these intoxicated Indians are carried back to their huts by relatively sober companions where they will recuperate, then rejoin the festivities, which continue unabated for three days and nights.*

75

CHICHA MAKING

CEREMONIAL DANCING

FESTIVAL MUSICIANS

INEBRIATION AT AN INNA FEAST

CRUISE SHIP • *Cruise ships from the United States sometimes schedule brief stops in San Blas. Seen here is a mola-maker's depiction of a luxury liner with its anchor down and its flags flying. Some passengers are descending the gangplank into a launch while others stand at railings or peer out of portholes. Indian boys dive for coins, emphasized by their exaggerated size, while Cuna men and women circle the giant ship in their cayucos in hopes of doing some brisk and profitable trading.*

SEA DOG • *This scaly demon,* perro del mar, *or sea dog, and his moon-faced, wild-haired rider look more like the principals of an Eskimo print than anything Cuna. It is sometimes difficult to specifically identify the mythical creatures repre-sented on molas for they are either not clearly defined in the maker's mind or there is an inability or unwillingness to discuss the matter. Cunas strongly believe in both good and evil spirits, but the darker ones seem to prevail on blouses.*

78

CUNA LORE, MYTHS,& LEGENDS

Ritual and the supernatural play an important part in the lives of all San Blas Indians. The Cunas' inner world is filled with good and evil spirits, taboos and superstitions. They believe in an almighty being who created people, then, distressed by their bad habits, punished them with three disasters—a great wind, loss of sunlight, and a huge flood—the very things that Cunas, vulnerable on their low-lying islands, fear most today.

DEATH MOLA WITH SKELETONS • *Like refugees from Mexico's Day of the Dead, these amiable skeletons perform a rickety Danse Macabre on this mirror-image mola panel. Such a beguiling idea would certainly amuse mola-makers and challenge their artistic skills with needle and thread. Skeletons show up on what are commonly known as "death" or "grave" molas (page 103). However, this one, made in the early 1960s, bigger than most (18" × 27"), seems much too large for an ordinary blouse. Although superior in quality to the general run of "airport art," it may have been made especially for the tourist market, which was just beginning to catch on at that time.*

MERMAID APPROACHING FISHERMAN & MERMAID CAPTURING FISHER-MAN • *The mermaid has two bad habits, according to Cuna lore. She causes trouble at childbirth and she plagues fishermen. Seen here are the front and back panels of a blouse showing on one side three mermaids approaching a lone fisherman who is tending his nets, unaware of impending danger. In the second panel the man seems doomed. He has been seized by the central mermaid while her evil companions have turned into black devillike creatures, gloating happily as his nets sink into the sea.*

DEVIL • *Cunas believe in a variety of evil spirits and fear them greatly. However, there seems to be little prejudice about using such images as mola designs. Seen here is an octopuslike creature clearly labeled Diablo, or Devil in English.*

79

DEATH MOLA WITH SKELETONS

MERMAID APPROACHING FISHERMAN

MERMAID CAPTURING FISHERMAN

80

ECLIPSE OF THE MOON LEGEND • *Cunas believe that eclipses are caused by a jaguar or a dragonlike monster that eats the moon. To prevent such catastrophes, an albino (called a Moon Child by the Cunas), because he has special powers and is protected by God, must go outside and shoot an arrow into the night sky. An arrow cannot go far, but its spirit travels to the dragon and stops it from biting the moon, which soon becomes full again. The legend is accurately portrayed on this exceptional mola, Achu Simutupalet. The dragon has attacked the moon and is eating it while an albino has climbed to a rooftop and is preparing to launch his magical arrow.*

DEER WITH BABY IN HAMMOCK

BIRD CARRYING FIGURE IN BAG

BIRTH-MYTH MOLAS • *The custom among Cunas is not to speak openly of sex, and children are kept innocent as to where newborn infants really come from. They are traditionally told by their mothers that babies are brought from heaven by birds, from the jungle by deer, or from the sea by dolphins. The first story is quite frequently translated onto molas and is shown here in two stylistically different versions. As can be seen, parents sometimes get more than they bargain for. The first airborne messenger seems to have bagged a monster while the bird below delivers a half-grown child. In the deer myth the animals look more like storybook giraffes as they carry the little stranger suspended between them in a hammock.*

BIRD DELIVERING BABY

Another legend tells of Tiolele, son of God, who cut down the great Tree of Life which resulted in the start of all flora, fauna, and waters of the world. God's greatest disciple, Ibeorgun, taught the Cunas their code of morality and instructed them in spiritual matters, medicines, festivals, and all else that governs their lives. He instituted a division of labor for men and women and made the first nose rings.

Cunas believe in spirits called Purbas who live in the eight levels of heaven and the underworld. Since each thing has its spirit, they are everywhere—in plants, animals, rocks, and trees. When a Purba is evil, it must be outwitted (page 79). Some Cuna men who possess mystical powers become Neles, playing a role similar to that of shamans in North American Indian cultures.

Circular fungus patterns found on leaves of the Sappi Karta tree are God's way of instructing artists. Medicine men use a broth from these leaves to bathe the eyes of women desirous of making beautiful molas. Juice from the fruit of the Cuna's Tree of Life, the *Genipa americana*, is applied to the skin of sick children, the dead, and girls at puberty in the belief that when the juice turns black the patient becomes invisible to evil spirits. Cuna women use this juice to paint black lines down their noses (page 62) for beauty's sake and with a lingering belief that it will ward off evil.

LEGENDS FOR FOLLOWING PAGE:

GIRL WITH FUNERAL BOAT • *San Blas islanders use especially decorated boats to transport their dead to the mainland for burial. This young girl holds a model of a funeral boat, complete with corpse and mourners, made from a coconut husk and decorated with scraps of colored cloth.*

DEVIL AND MAN • *One cannot be sure what the mola-maker had in mind when she stitched this grotesque creature—a cross between an octopus and a devil, both incarnations of evil in Cuna culture. The panel, which may be either political or mythical, obviously has more to it than meets the eye. Its action suggests struggle, for the man apparently is attacking the weird creature with a* machete. *Or maybe he is cutting it loose. In any event, the malevolent thing makes a marvelous graphic image.*

NIGHTMARE WITH OWL • *This blouse was made by a woman who lives on the island of Carti Suitupo, where story molas combine lively ideas with fine workmanship. She said it was meant to represent a bad dream she had recently had—that of a demonic owl swooping down to attack her. Here she shies away from its grasping talons. The blouse's reverse side is the "dream" mola pictured on page 212.*

FUNERAL BOAT WITH SOULBIRD • *This appears to be a modernized version of a Cuna soulboat with its symbolic banners, an American flag, and a Johnson outboard motor, one of the more practical mechanical aids the outside world has brought to San Blas. The soulbird, if, indeed, that is what this awesome hawk was meant to be, has taken on the familiar spread-eagled form of the United States emblem and, not without precedent, the passengers include a rather large dog.*

DEVIL AND MAN

GIRL WITH FUNERAL BOAT

84

NIGHTMARE WITH OWL

FUNERAL BOAT WITH SOUL BIRD

SOULBIRD AT JOURNEY'S END • *In Cuna religion a person's soul takes the form of a blackbird and, when death comes, follows the soulboat on its long journey to the Skyworld. The soulboat theme is a favorite among mola-makers of all ages and is reproduced in many different styles and variations. Less frequently seen are molas depicting the afterlife. This beautifully wrought example is, according to several informants, the soulbird after it has reached its heavenly destination. If this thought were intended, the idea combines elements of both Cuna and Christian religious teaching. The deified figure, seated with a bouquet of flowers, appears to be interviewing the newly arrived, wide-eyed bird while aides attend the soulboat's gaily fluttering banners. A more down-to-earth deduction suggests that this scene is meant to represent a modern funeral with a flower-covered bier amid customary Cuna trappings. Caution is advised in mola interpretation; even Cunas sometimes attribute different meanings to the same design.*

85

INDIGENOUS FLORA & FAUNA

SKELETAL FISH • *Double fish images are a common theme among mola-makers. Although hardly what can be called brilliant examples of the art, some of them do have wit and charm. While one side of a blouse usually depicts a skeletonized fish, as seen here, the reverse side shows the finny creature still plump and viable.*

Surrounded as they are by cool colors—a massive wall of emerald jungle fringed with green waving palms, a dome of sapphire blue sky, a broad expanse of subdued azure-green ocean, plus a flooring of brown sandy beaches and ash-gray earth bristling with dark tree trunks and dry thatched huts—it is no wonder that Cuna women sought the brightest hues for their mola blouses. Taking their cue from nature they became flaming flowers made more vivid by the dark coolness of the environment.

The rich tropical flora and fauna of San Blas served as the major source for artistic expression long before Cuna women developed the knack of appliquéing their clothing. We know from a 17th-century description that the Indians of Darien who were ancestors to the Cunas practiced body painting using stylized flower and animal designs (see quotation on page 52). Succeeding generations of artists have always turned to the wonderfully varied worlds of jungle and coral reef to record a never-ending procession of birds and beasts, flowers and fishes.

In mola art it is the feathered tribe that reigns supreme. Panama's jungles are filled with exotic birds, and Cunas have specific names for over sixty different varieties. Approximately one out of every five molas depicts a bird in one form or another.

Cunas make pets of wild songbirds, and small children are often seen walking nimbly about with parakeets perched on their heads or shoulders. Occasionally a baleful-eyed green and red plumaged parrot can be heard squawking words in Cuna dialect. Parrots are great favorites among mola-makers who stitch them in clusters on tree branches (page 92) or eating bananas with their Spanish name, *loro,* carefully appliquéd across the panel. Hummingbirds are pictured hovering over nectar-laden tropical flowers, and one popular design shows twin owls holding captured mice in their beaks. Hawks, eagles, and other soaring birds of prey are also represented.

Cunas keep chickens and usually portray them comically on molas. Hens lay multicolored eggs, and roosters strum battered guitars or sound off as tough top sergeants in army uniform, images taken, no doubt, from comic books and recruiting posters in a gleeful extension of the home-grown bird's career. Long-legged shorebirds lend themselves to even more ridiculous situations as mola-makers feature them wearing human clothing with heavy-rimmed spectacles balanced across scissorbeaks. Pelicans are caught in the act of devouring fish or seen as dancing skeletons.

Fish and other forms of marine life seem almost as popular with mola-makers as are birds. Some of the earliest pictorial blouses still in existence preserved from sixty or more years ago depict fish pattern molas. More contemporary subjects range from whales (page 70) to the lowliest shellfish. Sharks and manta rays (page 70) elicit involved scenes with fishermen harpooning from boats or

LEGENDS FOR FOLLOWING PAGE:

PELICAN FEEDING YOUNG • *Not only did the creator of this mola capture the timeless gesture of a mother pelican feeding her hungry fledgling, but she also introduced a chicken greedily eyeing a hapless frog and, not without humor, a relieved worm viewing the whole scene from a relatively safe distance.*

ALLIGATOR • *The alligator is called* caiman *in Spanish, a word derived from the Carib Indian language. These predatory monsters are found in large numbers along the banks of mainland rivers. Their jagged teeth are highly prized for making necklaces worn by Indian boys to ensure virility.*

BAT • *Bats, the familiar* murcielagos *or* raton viejos *of Latin-American life and literature, are well known in San Blas and are often used creatively in folktales and on molas. At night tiny oil lamps are kept burning in Cuna huts to prevent the evil* chupa de sangre *or vampire bat from entering and attacking the occupants.*

IGUANA • *Iguanas are rather large, clumsy-looking reptiles that inhabit the nearby jungles of mainland Panama. Besides providing interesting motifs for molas these harmless creatures, whose flesh is tender and tasty, also provide Cunas with a handy source of food.*

ALLIGATOR

PELICAN FEEDING YOUNG

88   BAT

IGUANA

ARMADILLO • *In this well-conceived and neatly wrought mola an armadillo is shown being grabbed by its tail— perhaps illustrative of some Cunu myth or legend. This is the customary method of catching these powerful but harmless vegetarians that provide toothsome food for the natives. In former times the skulls of these armored creatures were used to make ceremonial musical instruments. Cunas believe that when music is played, the virtues of the animal from which an instrument is made are introduced into the ceremony. Uchus, or carved wooden idols, are also occasionally found in the form of armadillos.*

89

SHORE BIRDS

HERMIT CRABS

PLANT FORMS

SHORE BIRDS, HERMIT CRABS, AND PLANT FORMS
• *Mola-makers seem to possess an intuitive ability to capture animal forms in their most characteristic shapes or movements. Anyone who has ever walked along an ocean shoreline should recognize the quick darting and turning movements of the various small beach birds. The tiny hermit crab with appendages reaching out from his recently purloined domicile is used here with satisfying repetition. The third subject, identified in Cuna dialect, resembles a common plant growing on the islands whose slippery seeds are collected for use as a soap substitute.*

90

celebrating their triumphant catches. Flying fish become fanciful creatures streaking over boats and men (page 71). Frogs, sea turtles, sea horses, and starfish are translated into abstract figures or elements in repeat pattern molas. Crabs and lobsters (page 105) merit entire panels and are stitched in meticulous detail, crustaceans as fit for the art lover's eye as for the gourmet's dinner table. The devilish octopus, symbol of evil to Cunas, gives the skillful mola-maker a chance to go wild with needle and colored cloth and, at the same time, memorialize the shortcomings of an unpopular political figure (page 212).

No creature seems too insignificant to find its way onto a mola. Insects, often greatly elaborated upon, have all been noted in stitchery. Butterflies and mosquitoes; common houseflies, bees, and wasps; ticks, scorpions, and beetles; spiders and ants; all are carefully studied and then worked into bright designs. Cunas have an open-mindedness about creatures that are considered repellent in societies less in tune with nature.

Any botanist would be delighted with the great variety of realistic and stylized plant forms that Cuna women use to decorate their mola blouses. Exotic tropical blossoms run the full color spectrum. A rich profusion of broad-leafed jungle plants, wild fruit trees, heavily laden coconut palms and palm nut trees, as well as all manner of plant life from land and sea are represented. Two motifs which figure prominently in Cuna mythology—the Tree of Life with its guardian spirit and the magical Sappi Kartai tree—inspire women to make beautiful molas. These and other familiar arboreal forms have been worked into both pictorial and abstract patterns that dazzle the eyes and confound the mind and at the same time jollify the spirit.

LEGENDS FOR FOLLOWING PAGE:

GIRL FEEDING PIGLET • *It is a common practice for San Blas Indians to keep pets and other domestic animals. This young woman has interrupted her sewing routine to feed a piglet from a baby's plastic bottle. The unusual detail in this scene, however, is her pet dog's nose painted with the traditional black line usually reserved for women and young girls. Although the gesture may have been a caprice, she probably felt that its magic would keep her dog safe from evil.*

PALM NUT TREE • *The palm nut tree grows throughout San Blas and is often used as a motif on Cuna blouses. Its traditional form is a crown of palmate leaves over-spreading an exaggerated X-ray view of the husk, revealing an interior arrangement of palm nuts. The reverse side (not shown) avoids repeating the same pattern by picturing two exotic, long-billed birds sipping nectar from a tropical blossom.*

PARROTS AND COATIMUNDIS • *Panama's local jungle provided the friendly wildlife seen communing on this delightful mola. Parrots and coatimundis, raccoon-like creatures found throughout Central America, are both familiar sights to Cunas who visit the mainland daily for supplies of food and water. This mola-maker thoughtfully avoided the usual balanced design by presenting her birds and beasts closely grouped and arranged asymmetrically in the branches of a tropical tree.*

NEST OF BABY LIZARDS • *A fine example of diligent workmanship, this mola shows a thoughtfully organized pattern of curled-up baby lizards as they might appear when hatching. It could also represent a scene from the underworld where, according to Cuna mythology, there is a specific enclosure for each and every creature.*

GIRL FEEDING PIGLET

PALM NUT TREE

PARROTS AND COATIMUNDIS

NEST OF BABY LIZARDS

PARASITIC INSECT • *There is no accounting for a mola-maker's taste in subject matter. A flea or similar mite can become as splendid as a peacock in the hands of a Cuna artist, and did, in this instance. Tropical insects have always been a nuisance, even a serious problem, to jungle inhabitants and have often influenced their migratory patterns or choice of village sites. Some historians speculate that one reason the Cunas moved, a hundred years or so ago, from Panama's lushly wooded mainland to the breezy* *offshore islands was to escape the relentless parasitic tormentors that infested their jungle abodes. The woman who created this design revealed an entomological curiosity or, at least, a wry sense of humor when she stitched this elaborate bloodsucking Siphonaptere, complete in anatomical detail and combining the characteristics of tick, louse, and flea, transforming it into a glorious example of sophisticated folk art. To balance her design, she added birds and her own mysterious version of winged insect forms.*

93

SCORPIONS, TURTLE FORMS, AND FISH WITH CAP • *Blood-sucking ticks and poisonous scorpions are not the most attractive of God's creatures, but one perceptive Cuna artist created a work of enduring beauty by stitching them onto her mola blouse. To most collectors the splayfooted, scarab-shaped creature below is no more than a primitive talismanic design but, according to others, it is an ancient turtle-within-a-turtle image representing the Cuna goddess of birth. Another mola-maker's tongue-in-cheek bestowal of a baseball cap on a colorful cichlid's head has made him the envy of his aquatic cousins as he haughtily cruises the crystal depths of his natural habitat.*

SCORPIONS

TURTLE FORMS

FISH WITH CAP

BIRDS IN A JUNGLE SETTING • *This unusual mola, showing birds perched on tree branches, was probably made in the 1930s. Although pictorial in content, its technique relates more to the construction of earlier abstract molas. There is an abundant variety of birdlife along the San Blas coast and in the mountainous jungles of the Darien, and Cuna women with their keen powers of observation are always on the lookout for new ways of presenting their favorite subjects.*

SPIDERS AND THEIR WEBS • *Proudly dated April 15, 1959, this mola carries a superfluous label, Araña, which means "spider" in Spanish. The choice of a "lowly" subject to adorn a woman's blouse, be it spider, reptile, or sea crab, is made without the negative connotations which would ordinarily prejudice someone from a society less in tune with nature. In this case, the artist responded to the complex harmony enjoyed in the silk-webbed world of arachnids by creating a work of exceptional beauty. Such detailed stitchery represents the loving care and persistent labor of many, many weeks.*

Commonplace animals have always been portrayed on molas, and since the Cunas' earliest experiments with the art of appliqué, these awkward renderings have exhibited an appealing directness and naïve beauty. As sewing techniques were perfected, they became more complicated, until this loose, informal quality was eventually replaced by more carefully conceived and intricately worked figures. By comparing the two animal motifs on the left side of page 55 with the armadillo on page 89, one can sense the evolutionary trend in mola art over the past half century.

A grand parade of native beasts has been observed on mola blouses over the years: from lowly rodents like rats, mice, bats (page 88), and squirrels; monkeys, sloths, coatimundis (page 92); wild and domesticated cats; and tapirs, they appear in primitive splendor. Nor have reptilians been neglected in this stitched-cloth menagerie; alligators, iguanas (page 88), lizards (page 92), and a fine sampling of snakes creep and crawl across these wonderful blouses.

The jungles of Panama abound in beautiful flowers and exotic creatures. Mola-makers, who are greatly influenced by the visual beauty of their immediate surroundings, take pleasure in rendering the familiar in elaborately stylized designs. Whether depicting birds, animals, insects, marine life, reptiles, or plant life, Cuna women have a marvelous way of capturing the character of their subjects. Sometimes this is done with bold simplicity, whereas at other times it is achieved by careful attention to form and detail.

Bird and beast, insect and plant, reptile and fish—they all come to life on colorful panels in a glorious tribute to the mola-maker's art and the place they call San Blas.

MOLA-MAKERS

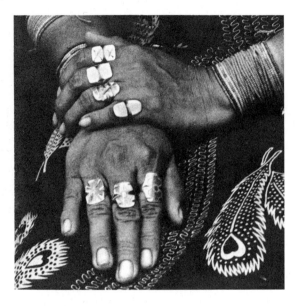

CUNA WOMAN'S GOLD RINGS

By now, a quarter of a century after they first began appearing in exhibition halls and the pages of popular magazines, molas are known to just about everybody concerned with folk art. Few, however, know anything about the artists who make them or, for that matter, where they come from. Cuna women are known, if at all, as those bizarre little Indians who use gold nose rings and wear brightly colored blouses appliquéd with cigarette ads and moon landing scenes. The fact that their unique needlework exists as anonymous art makes these artists even more remote.

Cuna women pursue simple and productive lives governed by tradition and enriched by ritual. Their art is strictly a woman's art which is intertwined with the total fabric of their being. They work compulsively with one or more unfinished designs always at hand, their sea island environment being conducive to an idyllic life-style which leaves plenty of time for creative stitchery. Their complicated appliqué technique is not practiced by neighboring Indian tribes or any other culture on earth.

CUNA WOMAN WITH
COIN NECKLACE

CUNA GIRL BABY • *The birth of a girl is much favored in Cuna society, which is basically matrilineal. Baby girls are adorned practically from birth with jewelry in the form of rings, nose rings, bracelets, and necklaces of shells, beads, gold, or gold substitutes. At a very early age mothers paint the traditional black stripe down the baby's nose. In another six years this child will begin learning the basic techniques of mola-making, but long before that time she will be as familiar with molas as her U.S. counterparts are with TV programs.*

100

YOUNG WOMAN WITH GOLD BIRD
AND TURTLE NECKLACE

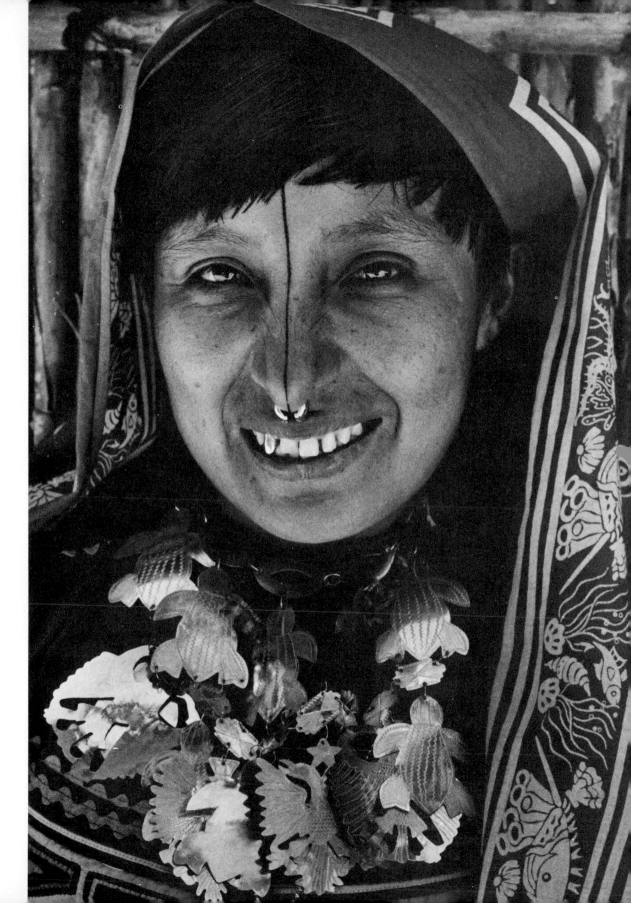

YOUNG GIRL WITH PRACTICE MOLA
• *At a very early age Cuna girls are taught the rudiments of mola-making. They use scraps of cloth from their mothers' sewing baskets to make little two-layered practice panels like the one pictured here.*

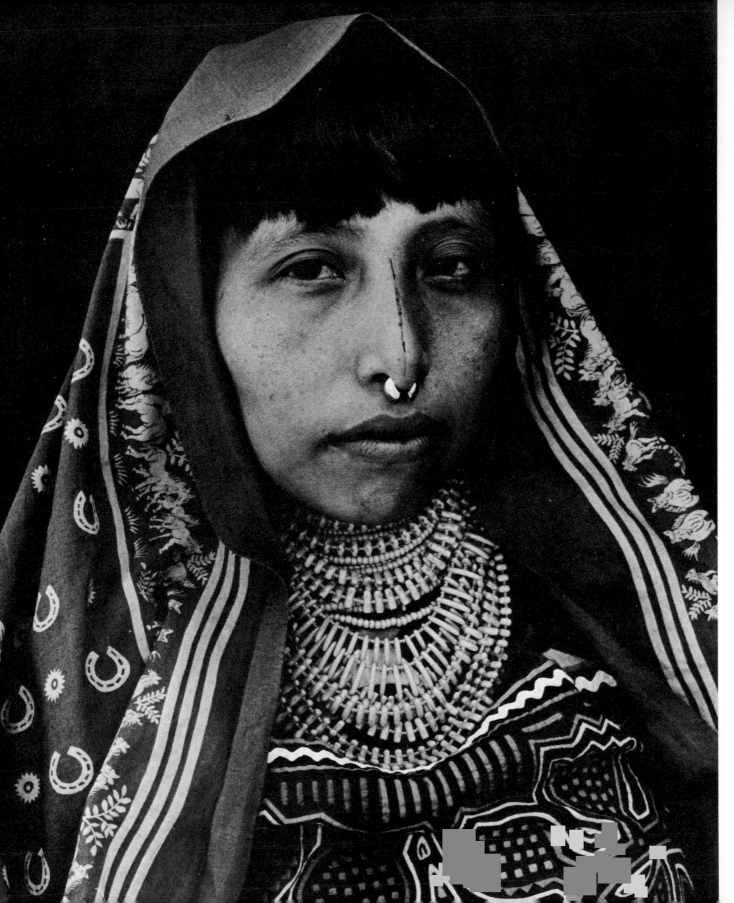

PORTRAIT OF A
CUNA ARTIST

SEA LOBSTER

WORK IN PROGRESS

AN ARTIST AND HER WORK • *The two molas featured here are the front and back panels of the same blouse. The top design, titled* Langosta del mar *depicts in fine detail the sea lobster found in abundance off San Blas Island reefs. The lower design is a skeleton conveniently folded back on itself to fit the space. Another work by the same artist is the amazing* Moon Landing *on page 152. The portraits show the creator of these designs in a formal pose and in a more relaxed moment working on a new mola blouse.*

DEATH MOLA

WOMAN DRESSED FOR
CHICHA FESTIVAL

YOUNG ALBINO SEWING A MOLA • *Occasionally young Cuna men, especially albinos who cannot work in the harsh tropical sun and are discouraged from marrying, choose the female way of life. They do women's work, including mola-making, and are fully accepted in the community. Pictured here is a young albino male sewing on a mola. His hair is cut in the feminine style and he is wearing a necklace and women's rings.*

PRESSING SUGARCANE • *Sugarcane is harvested on the mainland and brought by dugout to the islands to be crushed in simple but effective communal presses. The juice is used for general sweetening as well as for* chicha *(page 224). Pressure for operating the cane crushing mechanism is applied by one woman bouncing up and down on the end of a cantilevered pole while balancing herself with a long staff. Her companions feed the stripped canes through the press, twisting and moving them back and forth to extract every ounce of the sweet sticky juice.*

A CUNA WOMAN AND HER *PINGUINOS*
• *Well-known for her playful spirit and easy laughter, this young woman parted with her cleverly designed penguin mola (the two panels illustrated here) only after much debate and mock protestation. As soon as the deal was closed and payment made, however, she dashed into her hut and returned moments later sporting an almost-identical version of her delightful Antarctic pattern, which she promptly offered to sell. Showing both front and side views of a figure is a recent popular innovation on islands in the Rio Sidra area.*

PENGUIN MOLA, FRONT

PENGUIN MOLA, BACK

YOUNG WOMAN WEARING
PENGUIN MOLA

MOLA-MAKER FROM CARTI SUITUPO

DETAIL FROM DR. DOLITTLE MOLA

DR. DOLITTLE MOLA

A WOMAN AND HER WORK • *Carti Suitupo has many fine mola-makers who are particularly interested in creating designs from beyond their island world. This 29-year-old artist, known to her friends as Henry, is one of the best of them. Her work can be seen on page 156, Tarzan and His Friends; page 201, Dr. Dolittle; and page 224, Vodka Advertisement. Typically, she speaks no language but her own; however, she successfully tackles complicated English and Spanish phrases in her motifs. She is an innovator who seldom copies other women's molas but thinks up new and different ideas and then lavishes great love and care on executing them. The mola and detail on this page are the reverse side of the Dr. Dolittle blouse shown on page 201.*

MOLA-MAKER WORKING ON NEW BLOUSE

YOUNG WOMAN STARTING
MOLA PANEL

MOLA-MAKING WITH A SEWING MACHINE • *Machines have been commonly used in the islands for many years for sewing men's clothing or putting the component parts of a mola blouse together, and occasionally women use sewing machines to make molas. Though frowned upon by collectors, it is, nonetheless, a challenging proposition. Only linear designs or large sweeping curves can be practically managed, and even then the results are disappointing. It is doubtful that Cuna women will suddenly substitute sewing machines for their traditional needlecraft and, as some doomsayers insist, precipitate the rapid demise of mola-making.*

THE CANAL ZONE & U.S. MILITARY INFLUENCES

BOY SCOUT EMBLEM • *It would be difficult to find a more typically American image than this Boy Scout emblem with its world renowned motto "Be Prepared" inscribed beneath Uncle Sam's eagle and stars-and-bars shield. Mola-makers seem much attracted to insignia, military or civilian, and when a new one comes along, they rarely pass up the opportunity of incorporating it into their latest creations. The birds on this one are Cuna gratuities, but the four portraits may have been intended as photographs of honorary scouts.*

The opening of the Panama Canal in 1914 brought great changes to the Isthmus and since that time the Canal Zone has had a far-reaching influence on the lives of many San Blas Indians. With the installation of U.S. military bases came job opportunities and Cuna men soon gained reputations for honesty, a willingness to work, and the ability to learn quickly. Their jobs as cooks, orderlies, and maintenance men gave them a good working use of English and also taught some of them American habits. They began to buy low-priced manufactured products in the Zone to bring home when they visited their families on the islands. In this way a mass of strange and exciting visual material was made available to mola-makers.

Military subjects soon became popular as blouse designs. Insignia, American flags, recruiting posters, pictures of Army life, patriotic souvenirs, and nearly anything to do with the U.S. presence in Panama could be transformed into patterns of colorful stitchery. Airplanes, warships, and portable radar units (page 120) were sewn onto blouses and worn as casually as the Cunas' traditional bird and fish motifs.

During and after World War II the stream of material things from *La Zona* increased steadily in volume.

OLD MAN WITH MILITARY JACKET

• *Looking more like a carved wooden* uchu *than an actual person, this toothless old man stands on an upturned canoe and gazes placidly across the bay. His cap and military jacket suggest that he may have been one of the many Cunas who left San Blas to work in the Canal Zone. These men earn good pay as merchant seamen or working at various jobs in mainland cities, sometimes spending years before returning to the Islands with enough money to comfortably live out their days in, as they say,* paz y tranquilidad, *or peace and tranquility.*

RADAR LISTENING DEVICE • *This curious machine, mounted on wheels and controlled by wired operators, looks like a combination trolley car and army listening device. An examination by military experts could offer no positive identification except that it resembles a portable radar unit with parabolic reflectors. The figures inside, both male and female, seem to be waving to others stationed beside what are perhaps staff cars. Converging upon this huge piece of equipment are seven oddly shaped objects supposed to represent aircraft.*

UCHU BESIDE CUNA HUT • Uchus, *wooden figures used chiefly in medicine ceremonies, are carved by some of the Cuna men. The larger, more formidable* uchus, *like the one pictured here, are stationed beside doors as household guardians. Most are stiff and crudely carved, painted in raw, primary colors, often made to resemble some important historical personage whose power, it is believed, can be incorporated into the statue. During World War II, General Douglas MacArthur's reputation was known to Cunas through their contact with the military, and* uchus *were made in his image. Before that, sea captains and missionaries were so honored. Many of these figures are still carved wearing military caps and uniforms with painted insignia patterned after the MacArthur era. This door of Manuel Placio's hut is decorated with a star, a Panamanian flag, and a phoenix bird rising from a nest of flames.*

Cigarette packages, matchboxes, canned food labels, tools, whiskey bottles, and everyday objects from the outside world began appearing on molas. Boxing, baseball, basketball, and other American sports were introduced to the Cunas and quickly became subjects for women's blouse designs.

Although daily life in San Blas remains essentially as it was a hundred years ago, the gap between modern civilization and isolated island life has been bridged by exposure to Americans and the Canal Zone. Cuna economy is changing while mola-making has taken a new and exciting turn.

SCHOOLBOYS WITH AMERICAN FLAGS • *Eight properly attired schoolboys have lined up to help celebrate the November 3rd national Panamanian holiday with American flags and friendly waves. On the reverse side of this blouse (not shown), sixteen neatly uniformed girls, each shouldering a Panamanian flag, stand at attention while their leader raises their national banner. It is significant that the predominant colors used in this mola are red, white, and blue, the mola-maker's favorable comment on the close ties between Panama and the Canal Zone.*

JUNGLE WARFARE INSIGNIA • *This insignia of the American Jungle Warfare Training Center based at Fort Sherman in the Canal Zone had an irresistible appeal for one mola-maker. In her naïve way she managed to convey the symbolic essence of the deadly conflict—a handsome and heroic jaguar deftly subduing the enemy, pictured here as a poisonous-looking jungle snake with sinister red and black markings.*

UNITED STATES MILITARY EMBLEM • *A great variety of United States military signs and symbols are brought to San Blas by Cunas who work in "La Zona." Their womenfolk copy these emblems, elaborate upon their many forms, and use them for mola designs. The faulty lettering on this one reads: "Fort Sherman, Canal Zone."*

121

UCHU BESIDE HUT

SCHOOLBOYS WITH AMERICAN FLAGS

JUNGLE WARFARE INSIGNIA

U.S. MILITARY EMBLEM

ARMY RECRUITING POSTER • *The U.S. Army's reenlistment program during the 1940s and 1950s included a series of colorful posters that used animal caricatures to get its message across. These advertisements were displayed in prominent places around military bases and ultimately showed up on the San Blas Islands where they were inevitably converted into mola designs. This one features an eager-beaver paymaster or recruiting officer handing out greenbacks to military personnel. The random lettering reads "Your best protection—Steady income—Re-up Army."*

SPORTING EVENTS

SNORKELER • *Snorkeling is a vacation pastime for tourists in San Blas, but Cuna boys also use masks when diving for shellfish or when diving with spearguns for bigger game. This underwater scene shows a swimmer in action with face mask, snorkel, swims fins, and even a chain of air bubbles rising to the surface.*

Given their fine physiques and pride in athletic prowess, it is only natural that Cunas should enjoy a wide variety of sports. Some of the most popular are those introduced by the white man. These island Indians excell in team sports like baseball and basketball, both of which provide lively themes for molas.

Despite limited space, nearly every island has an outdoor basketball court. At almost any daylight hour and sometimes far into dusk young men can be seen enthusiastically shooting baskets and scrimmaging for the ball. Tournaments for these and other favored events are avidly followed by local fans, and trophies awarded to home teams are proudly stitched onto blouses.

While Cunas are noted for their peaceful natures, championship boxing bouts, promoted with much fanfare, hold a great attraction for those who work in the Canal Zone and Panama City. The graphics of that sanguinary sport turn up in the form of posters, cardboard cutouts, photographs, and a variety of printed matter which Cuna men carry home and which mola-makers convert into beautiful stitchery. It is not unusual for a popular boxer to appear posed in a fighting stance on a woman's brightly colored mola. Such outstanding prizefighters as world's champion

"Sugar Ray" Robinson, scrappy Carlos Ortiz, and Ismael Laguna all have been immortalized on these appliquéd blouses.

Water sports come naturally to the natives of San Blas. Much of their time is spent on the ocean, fishing or journeying back and forth to the mainland or from island to island in their dugout canoes. They are as much at home on the sea as they are on land. Impressed by their ability to handle small craft, John Mann, a former deep-sea diver from the U.S. who has dwelt among these people for many years, organized a sailboat race which has since become an annual event and subsequently been commemorated on mola panels. Activities such as diving, swimming, and snorkeling are also represented in both pictorial and abstract designs.

Interest in all sports contests has been capitalized upon by women who feature them on their blouses, thereby creating a distinct category of fascinating molas directly inspired by such diverse team sports as basketball, baseball, volleyball, and soccer, not to mention individual sports like boxing and wrestling, skiing and water skiing, bullfighting and cockfighting, plus a host of others, many of them seldom if ever witnessed firsthand by mola-makers.

It can be said that virtually all molas showing athletic events have been made in recent years, that is, since the period of World War II.

Sometimes a sports pattern is unique; more often it will have been copied from another woman's original design. Soon after the initial blouse has been finished, worn, and admired, its like can be seen in subtle variations on widely scattered islands for, if a design catches on, it spreads like wildfire. As time goes by, one is aware of a curious

LEGENDS FOR FOLLOWING PAGE:

CUNA SAILING RACE POSTER • *Colorful poster used by San Blas enthusiast, John Mann, to promote a sailboat race he organized among the Cunas.*

SAILBOAT RACE WINNERS • *The Cunas are excellent sailors and spend much time in their* cayucos, *or dugout canoes. This mola commemorates a* carrera de cayucos, *or boat race, and duly records the first, second, third, and fourth place winners of a contest which took place on March 14th, 1969, and is still remembered for its vigorous competition.*

BOXING MATCH PUBLICITY • *As part of the promotional buildup for forthcoming boxing matches, poster-painted life-size cutouts of the principle contenders—in this photograph a fighter named Hidalgo—are often displayed on the street corners of downtown Panama City.*

BASKETBALL GAME • *Basketball is a very popular sport in the San Blas Islands and occasionally becomes the inspiration for a superb illustrative mola. Distilled into this primitive design is the very essence of the game as well as intimate details which could tie it to a particular tournament.*

BASKETBALL PRACTICE • *It is interesting to compare the differences among molas using the same subject matter. Although patterns may be basically similar they can, according to the individual mola-maker's whim, vary widely in style and treatment. While the panel on the left emphasizes a basketball game in progress, this one seems to show players at practice and doing their warm-up exercises. The oversize ball has been quaintly decorated and the basket hoops have been turned as though they are being viewed from above.*

125

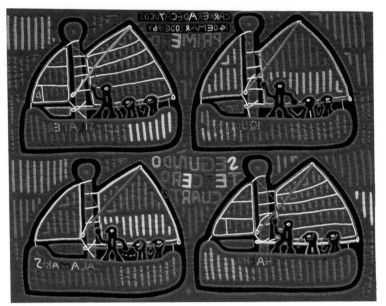

CUNA SAILING-RACE
POSTER

SAILBOAT RACE WINNERS

BOXING MATCH PUBLICITY

BASKETBALL GAME

BASKETBALL PRACTICE

BOXING MATCH KNOCKDOWN • *Although gentle people by nature, Cuna men take a keen interest in prizefighting and are seen regularly in attendance at boxing matches in Panama. This mola depicts a decisive moment in the squared ring—the referee counting at a knockdown as spectators crowd close to view the action. As with most good molas, this finely stitched panel is a labor of love, representing the artist's consummate skill and endless hours of sewing.*

PRIZEFIGHTER "SUGAR RAY" ROBINSON • *The two illustrations on this page are front and back panels of the same blouse. The design for this mola originated during "Sugar Ray" Robinson's reign as world's boxing champion. The caption indicates that the source was probably a news photo from an English language publication. It is interesting to note how much of the vitality of an action-packed contest has been preserved in this appliquéd handiwork.*

BOXING BOUT: LAGUNA VERSUS ORTIZ • *Ismael Laguna, a very popular fighter in Panama's boxing scene, is portrayed here with a formidable opponent, Carlos Ortiz. The smaller figure, outlined in blue and standing with upraised arms between them, is the referee; the ones in the lower corners represent members of the audience. Designs such as this one usually derive from the many colorful posters circulated prior to an important boxing match.*

transformation, for as the process of copy from copy continues, a design can so break down that it becomes far removed from the original, often so lost in abstraction that one has to search to see the relationship.

A dynamic feeling for action, coupled with the artist's sharp eye for detail, invests these pictorial sports molas with a vitality that elevates them into something quite beyond the ordinary and sets them apart in terms of contemporary folk art.

LEGENDS FOR FOLLOWING PAGE:

WRESTLING • *These bespectacled grapplers are performing wrestling's famous "airplane spin" while a spectator shouts encouragement and the hooded figure at right—"Grunt-and-Groan's" ubiquitous "Masked Marvel"—looks on.*

THE BULLFIGHT • *Bullfighting is taken seriously in Latin-American countries, and the imagination of this Cuna artist transformed the event into a beautiful mola. The matador is shown flourishing his cape as a highly decorated bull rushes past him. Both the matador's cape and "suit of lights" are covered with embroidered lettering, scrambled beyond comprehension because the majority of mola-makers neither read nor write; letters become simply design elements.*

BASEBALL • *This early 1950s baseball mola from the era of Joe Dimaggio and Phil Rizzuto has become a catchall for baseball paraphernalia. It commemorates the best pitcher (mejor lansador) and champion hitter in action. It also identifies bat (bate), shin guards (rodilleras), ball (pelota), and catcher's mask (careta). "Marilyn and Joe" refers to Dimaggio's well-publicized romance with movie actress Marilyn Monroe.*

COCKFIGHT • *Cockfighting has an avid following in most Latin-American countries. Anyone who has ever watched one of these sanguinary contests will recognize the furious grit-and-steel action generated by these embattled roosters. Aficionado or not, this mola-maker certainly caught the volatile spirit of the cockpit and smartly calculated the pecking order between two spurring-partners. Viewed from above this transformed arena is reminiscent of a recurring theme in mola designs, that of a turtle within a turtle, (page 94) described by some Cunas as a symbol of birth.*

129

WRESTLING

THE BULLFIGHT

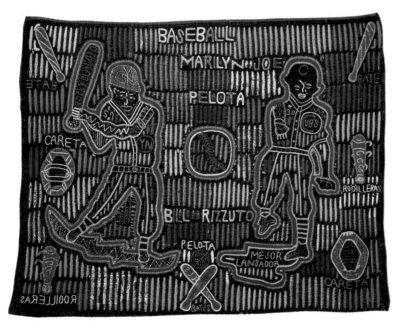

BASEBALL

COCKFIGHT

BASEBALL TROPHY • *In this instance the mola-maker proudly paid homage to the Cunas' victory in a baseball tournament. La Copa refers to the trophy cup. The inscription on the cup can be translated: "Amateur baseball tournament. For demonstrating the best sporting spirit. The Winner—San Blas."*

CHRISTIAN RELIGIOUS IMAGERY

SAINT FRANCIS AND THE BIRDS • *Molas based on Christian teachings are not always biblical in origin. Considering the Cunas' love of bird forms in their designs, it is only natural that they would be drawn to the story of Saint Francis of Assisi. This endearing mola, an ornithologist's delight, portrays the venerable saint at his notorious best, compassionately preaching the gospel to a congregation of birds and beasts.*

In the wake of the Conquistadors there came to San Blas an endless stream of pirates, assorted adventurers, sea captains, traders, and, inevitably, those harbingers of a new religion, Christian missionaries, who, if not directly responsible for the mola, certainly introduced one of its most exciting pictorial themes, that of biblical legend.

Teaching from the Old and the New Testament, the views presented by missionaries were a strange and radical departure from Cuna mythology. For those Cunas who came under their influence it was only natural that some of the major dramatic events of biblical literature would provide spectacular new ideas for molas.

From the very beginning mola-makers were attracted to the visual forms of religious symbolism and were quick to incorporate them into their stitchery. The cross, for example, which had previously been no more than a natural design element carried over from the Cuna's love of body painting, soon took on a new and special meaning. Heroic tales from Scripture were gradually assimilated and transformed into crude but exciting graphic designs for story molas. A proliferation of printed religious texts offered pictorial matter which mola-makers delighted in copying. Each woman interpreted the original in her own manner and style, the results of which were rendered to the best of her inspiration and competence.

The Old Testament story of Adam and Eve has broad appeal for mola-makers, treatment varing from simple to complex. Some versions depict the first couple confronting the serpent entwined in the branches of a flowering tree. Others show the entire Garden of Eden, animals, plants, and birds flying overhead, with the Devil disguised as a snake tempting Eve as she persuades her man to taste the forbidden fruit (page 135). An even more complex scene shows Adam and Eve, their nakedness modestly covered with girdles of jungle leaves, being driven from their Earthly Paradise by a wrathful land Lord who appears from a cloud bank, flaming sword in hand, to evict them.

Noah's ark has appeared on molas in various forms. A delightful and seldom found version worked in meticulous detail shows the prophet acting as accountant as he inscribes the names of assorted animals parading by and entering his none-too-seaworthy vessel (page 139).

When a mola-maker's imagination is fired by religious themes, the result can be The Creation (page 134), Samson Slaying the Lion (page 134), David and Goliath, Jonah and the Whale, the Three Wise Men (page 138), or the Annunciation. Each will be embellished to suit the maker's fancy and then, after weeks or months of tedious needlework, worn to a festival. After the garment has been roundly displayed and duly admired, it will become an everyday blouse because the artist by then will be occupied with another design planned to eventually replace the one she is wearing and to impress her competitors even more.

Two of the most frequently used religious themes are those illustrating the birth and death of Christ. Nativity scenes are usually worked out in considerable detail.

LEGENDS FOR FOLLOWING PAGE:

THE CREATION • *The Creation myth is a compelling theme for Cuna women. This panoramic vision comes directly from the Old Testament and shows God, at first on His celestial throne, then laboring in His magnificent seven-day marathon of creating the world. Presented in an illogical sequence are: heaven and earth; the light and darkness of day and night; land and sea; the sun and moon and stars; fish and fowl; beasts of the field; and man and woman.*

SAMSON KILLING THE LION • *In spite of the two monkeys and what appears to be Tarzan, this is, according to its creator, a biblical Samson killing the lion. Both Tarzan and Bible stores are frequently used as mola designs, so it is possible that the two images were confused.*

THE JUDGMENT • *This cosmoramic design, loaded with Christian symbols, may have been based on an illustration from a religious publication for it has all the elements of a Doomsday pageant. There is no escaping the all-seeing Eye of God, which dominates this bird's-eye view of Judgment Day and sends light rays of discovery in all directions. The extended arm of Saint Michael is holding a set of scales as a roster-toting angel contends with the Devil for souls of the dead. The wily Prince of Darkness is attempting to set the scales off balance in order to collect his bounty of miserable sinners, but they are mercifully tipped in favor of the godly. A hand with a quill pen is recording names in an eternal ledger while below, self-contained in transparent globes, are vignettes of heaven and hell. The bearded godlike figure holding the cross above is labeled* Jesu Cristo, *or Jesus Christ. A strictly Cuna innovation is the addition of several soulbirds rising heavenward through billowing clouds.*

133

DETAIL FROM SAMSON MOLA

THE CREATION

SAMSON KILLING THE LION

THE JUDGMENT

134

THE GARDEN OF EDEN • *Eve, encouraged by both the Serpent and the Devil, picks forbidden fruit from a fanciful apple tree and presents it to a gullible Adam who is accompanied by a dwarf deer, like those found in Darien jungles and often kept as pets on the San Blas Islands.*

The legend stitched into the top border translates: "Chachardi, Mulatopo, the Devil with Adam and Eve." This mola was made in Mulatupo Sarsardi (which means Vulture Island in Cuna dialect), a village near the Colombian border, where Christian missionary influence is strong.

135

CRÈCHE WITH ANGELS • *Nativity scenes make their annual appearance in Panama's numerous churches, and it is not unlikely that something of the kind would show up on the San Blas Islands. Tiny models of tableaux like this one make excellent gifts for the faithful and fine subjects for mola-makers as well. The idea for this crèche may have come from a Christmas card, but the flowers, stars, and fluttering angles are pure Cuna.*

ADAM AND EVE • *Cuna Indians have their own Creation myths, but the story of Adam and Eve, brought to them by early travelers and missionaries, captured their imaginations and has become a persistent theme on religious molas. Although a much simpler statement than the example on the preceding page, all the essentials of that familiar story are here—the sinister serpent, the forbidden fruit, and the principle characters, duly chastened and sporting their latest "fall" fashions.*

Although similar in subject matter, individual styles and treatment cause the blouses to differ distinctly one from another (pages 138 & 140). The Christ Child, always the dominant figure, is generally shown nestled in a manger or held securely in its mother's arms, more often than not emanating an embroidered aura of golden light. Besides Madonna and Child, a bearded Joseph, the Three Wise Men, and a variety of animals, domestic and otherwise—many of them totally foreign to the geographical setting of Bethlehem but, nonetheless, naïvely appropriate in style and intention—form a circle around the newborn infant. On less studied versions, the Wise Men and animals are often left out altogether.

Molas depicting the Crucifixion conform closely to a standard motif with Christ on the cross surrounded by symbols of the Passion. They are most often made with exceptional skill and care. It would almost seem that unless a woman feels confident that she can really make a beautiful mola she will not attempt this subject. The fronts and backs of Crucifixion blouses frequently show different versions of the same basic design. This is especially true of those made in the Carti area of San Blas. On one side Christ, nailed to the cross, is flanked by four mourning figures. On the reverse side the mourners are replaced by symbols of the Passion—ladder, cock, coins, etc.—depicted in minute detail (page 142). Usually the letters INRI are inscribed above the crucified figure, and occasionally one encounters a mola with the legend "Christ is dead" written in Cuna dialect. It is curious that, among many primitive peoples, Christ most often appears as a black man, although mola-makers also color him white or yellow, even green, blue, or pink.

LEGENDS FOR FOLLOWING PAGE:

BIRTH OF CHRIST • *The birth of Christ is a recurring theme on religious molas. This scene shows the Holy Mother with her blessed infant on a pallet of straw in the manger, surrounded by sheep and cattle. The three Magi who have traveled from afar following a brilliant star have arrived at their destination and are offering fine presents to a radiant infant Jesus. Angels appear in flight overhead while, for no apparent reason, the heads of a horse and a big black cat have been isolated in circles amid a flurry of disjointed lettering.*

MADONNA AND CHILD • *This unusual Madonna-and-Child mola shows Mary in richly decorated robes emanating a radiance that blossoms into a dazzling display of Christian crosses. The figures beyond her aura are depicted in various attitudes of praise. The lettering surrounding her halo is in Spanish and reads* Nuestra Madre, *or* Our Mother.

THE THREE WISE MEN • *The story of the Three Wise Men has been firmly implanted in the minds of Christian Cunas and is often repeated regardless of the season. Here they appear turbaned and on horseback, bearing their precious gifts to the newborn babe in Bethlehem. Although not companion pieces, and discovered in collections thousands of miles apart, this and the above mola are closely related stylistically. Neither horses nor donkeys (not, for that matter, camels, the traditional mounts of the three original star-trekkers) are found in the San Blas Islands but even so Cuna artists have an uncanny talent for catching the character of the animals they depict on molas.*

DETAIL FROM NATIVITY SCENE   BIRTH OF CHRIST

138   MADONNA AND CHILD   THE THREE WISE MEN

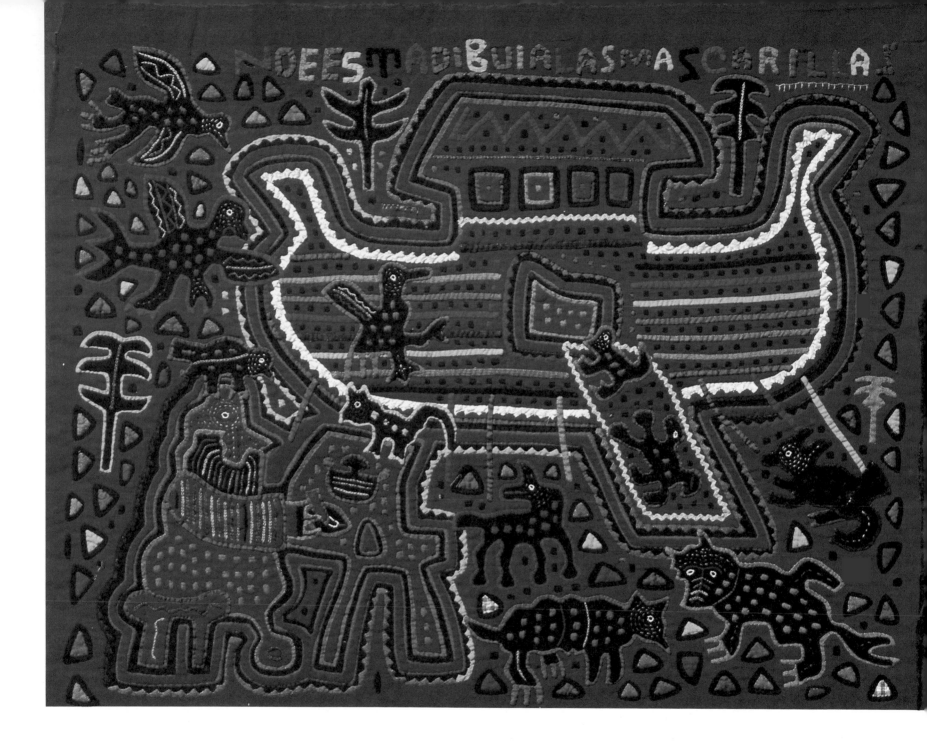

NOAH'S ARK • *The biblical epic of Noah's ark and the Flood has captured the imagination of Cunas, who also have a deluge story in their mythology. In this graphically rendered scene a bearded Noah sits at his desk keeping the record straight as an assortment of animals enter the zoological vessel.*

NATIVITY SCENE

ANNUNCIATION

ANNUNCIATION AND NATIVITY SCENE
• Depicted here are both front and back panels of an early 1970s mola blouse showing the Annunciation, and the birth of Christ. Translated, the Spanish lettering reads, "Holy Mary, Our Mother" and "Jesus is born in Bethlehem." The Nativity scene is illuminated by a modern oil lamp similar to those used in Cuna huts for sewing at night. While the work outside each circle is ordinary, the figures within are carefully conceived and lavishly embellished with fine stitchery, suggesting that they may have been copied from Christmas cards, a religious publication, or a magazine advertisement.

LEGENDS FOR FOLLOWING PAGE:

SAN BLAS ISLAND CHURCH • A far cry from the grandiose cathedrals which sometimes appear on Cuna blouses, this tiny Methodist mission on the island of Acuatupu is much closer to the kind of church that most San Blas Indians know.

ORNATE CATHEDRAL • Copied, no doubt, from a book or magazine illustration, here is a masterful study of a cathedral with domed bell towers and Romanesque arches, unlike any house of God ever seen in the San Blas Archipelago. This elaborately worked panel is remarkable for its fine stitchery and pictorial quality as well as its combined use of traditional mola techniques and rich embroidery. The airborne global objects are probably illuminated paper balloons sent aloft during religious festivities.

CRUCIFIXION WITH PASSION SYMBOLS & CRUCIFIXION WITH MOURNERS • In recent years in the Carti and Mandinga areas of San Blas, religious molas have appeared showing two variations of the Crucifixion scene. On one side Christ is flanked by four mourning figures. On the reverse side these figures are replaced by symbols of the Passion. Crucifixion blouses are usually richly colored with orange, red, and pink predominating, combined in ways not ordinarily found on other molas. Blouses of this type are greatly appreciated by their makers since they involve much work and are almost always of a superior quality.

SAN BLAS ISLAND CHURCH

ORNATE CATHEDRAL

CRUCIFIXION WITH PASSION SYMBOLS

CRUCIFIXION WITH MOURNERS

PRIMITIVE CRUCIFIXION SCENE • *This crucifixion scene came from Mulatupo, which lies at the lower end of the San Blas Islands chain, down toward Colombia, where fine molas are not as frequently found as in the Carti or other more accessible areas. The woman who made this mola said that she had put much time and labor into it. The lettering, "Papmachi Purkuis," at the top above the classical INRI, is in Cuna dialect and translates "Christ is dead." Cuna words are only occasionally found on molas, and those are usually on designs of a purely indigenous nature. Another unusual feature is the treatment of the figures at Christ's feet. Compared with the stiffly stylized mourners on most Crucifixion molas, these have an almost Picasso-esque vitality.*

143

MANNED FLIGHT

The " Minerva."

OLD BALLOON PRINT • *The end of the eighteenth century and the beginning of the nineteenth brought many strange and wonderful balloon schemes. In 1804 a Flemish physicist and aeronaut, Etienne G. Robertson, published in Vienna and subsequently in Paris, a plan for a giant balloon designed to tour the world. He called it " 'La Minerva,' an aerial vessel destined for discoveries and proposed to all the Academies of Europe." His marvelous machine was to be 150 feet in diameter, made of unbleached silk and coated with India rubber. It could accommodate 60 persons and would be capable of carrying 150,000 pounds. The globe would sustain a boat providing all passenger conveniences as well as guaranteeing safe return in case the flight ended over water. Such an extravagant project, if it was indeed serious, was unacceptable to the savants of that time; having met with satire and derision, the plan was finally abandoned.*

stitched history of man's love affair with flying can be traced graphically on molas. Examples range from the legendary Icarus to the Age of Rocketry. Some interpretations are so primitive in concept that the viewer must look closely to make out whether they are aircraft at all, whereas others are so detailed and sophisticated that one wonders how they were ever translated into stitchery.

The portrayals that are obviously first-hand accounts of sightings sometimes tend toward the fantastic; for example, there are still Cuna women who insist that airplanes are giant insects because they buzz and resemble them when seen from a distance (page 152).

Mola-makers lavish much time and care on their flying machines. Some designs are of schematic propeller-driven transport planes with cutaway sections showing the interiors as Indian artists imagine them, and passengers sitting at tables while stylized pilots man the controls.

This preoccupation with aircraft dates, along with other modern-day acculturation subjects, from the time of World War II. Before then few planes were seen in San Blas. Today, the drone of small aircraft is heard daily, particularly over the northern islands where many of the flight molas are made.

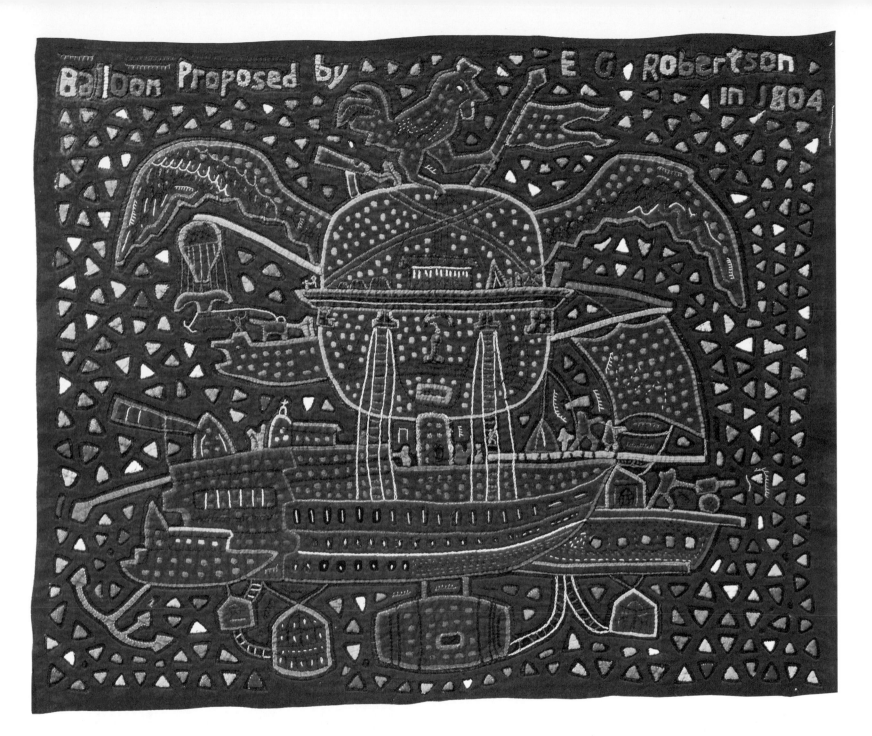

ROBERTSON'S FANTASTIC BALLOON, "THE MINERVA"
• *This extraordinary mola, stitched in minute detail, was copied from an early nineteenth-century French engraving, more than likely reproduced as a book illustration. The lettering reads: "Balloon proposed by E. G. Robertson in 1804." The mola-maker was obviously fascinated by her subject, for she lavished an incredible amount of care and fine needlework on its production. The source, which is pictured opposite, was taken from an 1870 book called* Wonderful Balloon Ascents, *translated from the French of F. Marion.*

145

FOUR PRIMITIVE AIRPLANE DESIGNS

• *For every sophisticated airplane design found on a mola there are half a dozen others that look like rejects from an incompetent engineer's drawing board. The magnificent men in these jerry-built flying machines seem to have taken off in a fog of artistic ingenuity and bizarre incomprehension.*

TRI-MOTOR BOMBER

146   FIGHTER PLANE

SINGLE-ENGINE AIRCRAFT

PASSENGER PLANE

LEGENDS FOR FOLLOWING PAGE:

SIKORSKY HELICOPTER • *When the artist portrayed this helicopter she unwittingly paid homage to the giant of the industry, Igor Sikorsky, whose name appears on the fusilage. Although her fancy obviously favored aircraft, on this, the reverse side of her blouse, she expanded her repertoire of strange machines by including a one-man submarine. The miscellaneous assortment of wildlife was added merely to fill up space.*

AIR FORCE PLANE • *A four-engined air force transport plane, complete with personnel, insignia, and registration numbers, dominates this military motif. Surrounding it is an odd blending of San Blas' indigenous fauna and unfamiliar vehicles from the outside world—a helicopter operated by a foxy pilot with a big bad wolf in tow, a stubby staff car, and what appears to be an amphibious half-track with a crew*

member catching a fish. This and the Sikorsky helicopter design are front and back panels of the same blouse. They aptly demonstrate the often surreal effects of acculturation.

BOY WITH MODEL PLANE • *Like small boys everywhere, this Cuna youngster is fascinated by airplanes and enjoys showing off the unwieldly balsa wood model carved by his father.*

NAVY BLIMP • *A United States Navy Blimp with mooring lines attached is being maneuvered into position for a landing while its sister ship hovers in the background. The mooring tower, ground personnel, and crudely silhouetted circling planes indicate that the scene is an airfield. The flag wavers are probably members of a welcoming committee for dignitaries aboard.*

147

SIKORSKY HELICOPTER

U.S. AIR FORCE PLANE

BOY WITH MODEL PLANE

NAVY BLIMP

OLD-TIME BIPLANE • *Whatever message may have accompanied this vintage airplane has been hopelessly scrambled by the artist's use of lettering simply for its decorative effect. The plane itself, an old-style propeller-driven biplane of dubious manufacture, sports military insignia on its wing tips. The occupants appear to be trailing inscribed banners promoting, perhaps, some advertising scheme or instructing prospective voters in an upcoming political contest. The subject matter, technique, large size (16½ inches x 22 inches), and coarse quality cloth are all clues to indicate that this mola probably dates from the 1930s.*

LANDING ON JUNGLE AIRSTRIP

SMALL PLANES TO SAN BLAS • *A fleet or
small aircraft leaves Paitilla airport shortly
after dawn each morning to fly over the
rugged Cordilleras to the dozen or so landing strips scattered along the San Blas coast.
Besides cargo and tourists, the passenger list
includes affluent Cunas who use these
planes regularly for interisland and Panama
City travel. In the photograph a cluster of
Indians crowds around a newly arrived
plane as mail is handed out. These tiny
aircraft may look like toys against the vast
jungle landscape, but they are a vitally
important link between the Cunas' world
and the civilized world outside.*

A few years ago parachutists became a vogue for mola-makers, and for a while figures in rigs no safety inspector could possibly approve were seen floating down the fronts of mola blouses.

Overstuffed blimps have also been immortalized in fine appliqué. These curious monsters may have been seen from time to time, perhaps on the mainland or during military maneuvers. More likely this attractive visual idea came directly from a picture magazine brought home to appease the insatiable curiosity of Cuna womenfolk.

After airplanes had become somewhat commonplace, helicopter molas began to appear, and, during the past decade or so, whirlybirds have equaled winged aircraft in mola popularity, worked in all shapes and sizes.

Hot-air balloons are found now and then, but so far none has matched E. G. Robertson's fantastic creation, "The Minerva" (page 145). How this wonderful source illustration (page 144) ever got to San Blas is a mystery which will probably never be solved. One likes to think that a daring balloonist once soared over the islands, but a printed source is much more likely to have inspired the current spate of balloon molas.

As manned flight has progressed, so molas depicting the subject have kept pace. It was not long after Gemini 5 had circled the earth that the event was commemorated on molas (page 153). The same thing happened with the Armstrong-Aldrin moon flight (page 152) appearing for a while throughout the Carti area. The amusing irony of it all is that most Cunas think the space program is no more than a fine fable. They still believe that the moon during eclipse is devoured by a monster which must be shot by a "Moonchild," or albino, or the world will be darkened forever (page 81).

LEGENDS FOR FOLLOWING PAGE:

INSECT AIRPLANE • *Confusion about aircraft is not uncommon in the minds of some Cunas. This artist's concept was that of a great droning insect disgorging parachutists. The design may have been inspired originally by United States military training exercises along the Panamanian coast.*

NAVY HELICOPTER • *United States Navy helicopters range far and wide over the coastal waters of Panama. The creator of this mola took a more realistic view than the one who represented an aircraft as a huge insect. She also caught the flimsy feeling of tiny "choppers" in this one, whose original may well have visited her island at some time or other. The bombs and armored vehicle suggest a military mission, although more than likely they were copied from an illustrated periodical.*

MOON-LANDING • *One of the most publicized moments in history, Neil Armstrong and "Buzz" Aldrin's July 20, 1969, planting of an American flag on the moon, is commemorated with amazing detail in this ultramodern Apollo adventure design. Since the moon figures so prominently in Cuna myth and legend it is little wonder that the account of man's first lunar flight should excite mola-makers. Note what careful attention has been paid to the astronaut's suit and the Apollo 11's lunar module, Eagle, with its Rube Goldberg antennae and landing pods extended for stabilization. At the left is a seismic package to detect lunar tremors. Celestial bodies illuminate the sky while a command module circles overhead. The source for this mola was undoubtedly a magazine or newspaper photograph.*

INSECT AIRPLANE

NAVY HELICOPTER

DETAIL FROM INSECT
AIRPLANE

MOON LANDING

152

SPACE CAPSULE • *All the activity of a successful splash-down and rescue operation is captured in this spaceflight mola. Frogmen, rubber raft, and helicopter with lines attached attend the returning astronauts. The space capsule's side has been cut away to show its interior with occupants preparing to disembark. The upper lettering commemorates "The North American Astronaut, Leroy Gordon Cooper"* who, *with Charles Conrad, took off in Gemini 5's Titan rocket on August 21, 1965, and returned to earth eight days later. Spaceflight themes were much in favor among mola-makers during that period of the Space Program, particularly in the Carti area where workmanship was equal to the challenge and resulted in some very high-quality molas.*

153

ILLUSTRATIONS FROM BOOKS, MAGAZINES, ETC.

PRIMITIVE TARZAN • *Tarzan, son of the late Lord and Lady Greystoke and foster child of an undiscriminating family of apes, has long been a favorite subject for mola-makers, but few have endowed him with such rambunctious vitality as this one. In this version, the famous Ape Man in his savage setting looks more simian than human. This mola, compared to the Tarzan mola on page 156, is quite primitive, but what is lacking in finesse is made up in sheer exuberance. You can almost hear Tarzan's eerie jungle yell as he and his faithful friend, Cheetah, seem about to leap right off the panel.*

The introduction of printed pictorial matter has exerted a vital influence on mola-makers. A few books, mostly religious, would have been seen in some areas of San Blas before the 1930s, but at that time their effect on mola-making was negligible. By the 1940s communications between the islands and Panama were well established and outsiders visited much more frequently, these brief contacts helping to open a whole new world for mola-makers.

Although only about one blouse design in fifty comes directly from a book or magazine illustration, as a group these are a most fascinating element in mola art. It must be remembered that most Cuna women neither read nor write and very few can speak words in Spanish or English—yet they seek out printed matter in both languages for designs. The mola-maker's response to the printed page is purely visual, and when words or phrases are incorporated into a mola design, it is usually done without knowing what any word means. The disparate variety of graphic material which has come their way ranges from medical diagrams to comic book scenes (pages 161 & 162) and from ancient history (page 158) to children's stories (pages 166 & 167).

This material reaches the San Blas Islands in many ways. Some proselytizing missionary groups rely heavily on illustrated religious tracts to help get their message across to prospective converts, and their dramatic images appealed strongly to Cuna artists. As more islands started schools, younger children were instructed through gaily colored picture books. Mothers often used these universal

LEGENDS FOR FOLLOWING PAGE:

WESTERN HORSEMAN MAGAZINE
• *Cover of the September, 1966, issue of* Western Horseman *magazine which inspired the mola at left.*

MOLA FROM WESTERN HORSEMAN MAGAZINE COVER • *Many Cunas have never seen a real horse. There is no need for such large animals in the San Blas Islands; the Indian's* cayuco *serves as both transportation and workhorse. Nonetheless, the idea of riding such a beast is daringly romantic, and mola-makers have great fun depicting equestrian events. A quick glance at the magazine cover from which this design was copied proves what liberties a Cuna's freehand artistry can take with a subject and still keep it within recognizable bounds. All the important elements are here—the elongated horse with its flowing tail, the mounted not-so-tall-in-the-saddle hombre wearing old Spanish-type spurs, and the cluster of foreign flags denoting an international gathering for western horsemen—but the artist's concept has distorted them almost beyond comparison. A close inspection also shows that two flags' escutcheons have been slyly changed into Cuna bird motifs. The lettering here was the surest clue to identifying the source for this pictorial panel.*

SALOON SCENE FROM THE OLD WEST • *Some of the cowpokes are whooping it up down at the Trail's End Saloon and a scraggly bunch of trail-weary, bow-legged waddies they are as they belly up to the old watering trough for three fingers of the jolly barkeep's red-eye. One rough-and-ready type has his shootin' iron slung low and another staggers away under a full load of tanglefoot. The figure who has dropped to one knee in true western movie fashion and seems to be holding his arm as though he has been shot is probably no more than half-shot and that from the booze he's been guzzling. Mexico's national emblem, an eagle with a snake scissored in its beak, crowns the mirrored backdrop with South-of-the-Border cantina flair. However, the general setting identifies the establishment as one right out of the pages of the wild and woolly west. Because of this mola's remarkable detail and true-to-life quality, one can assume that the Cuna artist must have copied it from a print of some kind, perhaps a sheet of calendar art, a pulp western's cover, an old chromolithograph, a movie poster, or even a liquor advertisement.*

TARZAN AND HIS FRIENDS • *Edgar Rice Burroughs's lord of the jungle is vividly portrayed here with some of his beastly cronies. Famous the world over for his manly physique and marvelous way with wild animals, Tarzan has thoroughly captured the imaginations of jungle-oriented Cunas. It hardly matters whether this colorful panel was inspired by a movie poster or copied directly from the pages of a Tarzan comic book; what is significant is the artist's treatment of her subject and the superior quality of her workmanship. Her astute sense of color and design, her fine use of stitchery, and her wry sense of humor are all apparent in this handsome mola.*

"WESTERN HORSEMAN"
MAGAZINE

MOLA FROM "WESTERN HORSEMAN" MAGAZINE COVER

SALOON SCENE FROM THE OLD WEST

TARZAN AND HIS FRIENDS

SCIENCE FICTION MAGAZINE COVER • Cunas are *fascinated by the unusual. They love science fiction and other highly imaginative illustrations that pique their curiosities and provide lively content for their molas. This fantastic scene shows an adventurous figure emerging from a tangle of weird jungle plants while firing a Buck Rogers-type* ray gun at a disembodied hand. The 10¢ price tag indicates *that it was probably reproduced from the cover of a lurid pulp magazine. Two such publications, Street and Smith's* Unknown *and* Unknown Worlds, *were popular during the late 1930s and early 1940s, but this mola probably came along a decade or so later.*

CLASSICAL MAP OF EUROPE • *One learns to expect the unexpected in mola designs, but a detailed classical map of Greek colonies in Europe comes as a total shake-up. Maps of Panama, on the other hand, occasionally do turn up on Cuna blouses. The source for this cartographic surprise must have been an illustration from an atlas, a world geography, or history book, or a volume on ancient Greece which somehow fell into the hands of the San Blas islanders. All indications are that this work, which showed signs of much wear and fading when it was collected more than a decade ago, probably dates from the late 1940s.*

158

TOM SAWYER • *Mark Twain's* Tom Sawyer *is not unknown to Cunas as many children's classics have reached San Blas schools in translation, but this most memorable fence-painting scene could just as well have been taken secondhand from a paint company's advertisement (perhaps Dutch Boy, for the basket-carrying figures appear to be wearing wooden shoes). It seems to be saying, "Look, instead of just one apple, we'll each give you a whole basketful if you'll only allow us the pleasure of using that wonderful brand of paint."*

THE VIKING SHIP • *This Viking vessel, proudly sporting its carved prow and full sail emblazoned with a spread-winged bird, is a magnificent example of fine mola-making. The intricate stitching is all but invisible, the pictorial content is clear and provocative, and the artist has added hundreds of minuscule cutouts to enhance the overall design. A terrible three-headed dragon hovers above the boat as though in close pursuit, but since the occupants seem unconcerned it may have come along as their guardian spirit. These stalwart Norsemen, in spite of their fiercely horned helmets, seem less intent on plundering villages than they are on enjoying a blue-water outing. Blouses with this same design showed up several times in the Porvenir area during the early 1960s, always neatly executed and of superior quality. A book or some other printed source could have prompted this seapiece, but more than likely it was a spin-off from a Kirk Douglas movie called* The Vikings, *which had played in Panama a few months before.*

ALI BABA AND THE FORTY THIEVES • *This story mola, complete with authentic costuming, was obviously copied from a picture, presumably from one of the many illustrated versions of* The Arabian Nights. *It makes vibrantly graphic what appears to be the crucial and most memorable scene in the classic tale of "Ali Baba and the Forty Thieves"—the devoted female slave, Morgiana, thwarting a plot to murder her master by pouring boiling oil into each of thirty-seven great jars and killing the robbers hidden within. To be sure, the turbaned figure shown sprinkling grains of something through a sifter is at variance with the story, which could indicate that the source was an advertisement of some kind, itself a copy once removed from the original illustration. It is not unusual, however, for mola-makers to take liberties with their material or to sacrifice accuracy by introducing totally unrelated elements from other pictorial sources.*

tales as sources for lighthearted designs. The Little Red Hen on page 164 is one such example.

Comic books and American magazines acquired by menfolk working in the Canal Zone were also coveted for their colorful contents. Everything from *Western Horseman* (page 156) to *Colliers, Unknown* (page 157), and *National Geographic* were studied for possible design ideas. Spanish and English language newspapers, with pictures of current events, were always welcome. An occasional visitor might leave behind tourist brochures, a newspaper, and other attractive printed matter, unaware that it would be treasured by women who seldom ventured beyond their own island horizons. It is also possible that mola enthusiasts may have purposely left printed images, hoping they would later turn up on blouses.

With better health care came clinics, instructive posters, and literature with medical and anatomical illustrations. TB has been a major killer among San Blas Indians and the detailed diagrams of lungs used in poster campaigns to fight this disease have not gone unnoticed (page 160). At

THE RESPIRATORY TREE • *In recent years some degree of modern medical treatment has become available in a few of the San Blas Islands and with it have come medical books, charts, and posters warning against disease. Indians are highly susceptible to tuberculosis and other lung ailments, so it is not surprising that this diagrammatic drawing of "the Respiratory Tree" intrigued one Cuna artist enough for her to spend many weeks sewing the detailed design of human lungs onto a blouse to be proudly worn at some upcoming feast. Parts of the entire respiratory system, consisting of larynx, windpipe, both right and left lungs, and bronchial tubes, have all been explicitly labeled in Spanish.*

DETAIL FROM THE VIKING SHIP

THE VIKING SHIP

"ALI BABA AND THE FORTY THIEVES"

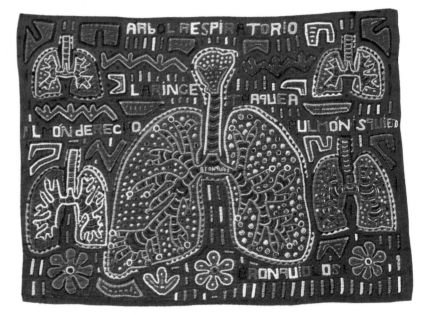

THE RESPIRATORY TREE

HAWKMAN BLOUSE • *Any 1960s comic book fan will recognize this masked winged figure as the intrepid Hawkman, hero of many a bizarre adventure in fantasy land. A seemingly insignificant subject has here been worked into an exquisite mola, which must have taken months to complete. The artist had trouble with her perspective and anatomy, not to mention the inverted* w *in her title, but the portrayal is graphic enough to suggest that it came directly from a sensational comic book cover. As a change of pace, she chose for the back panel a rum bottle label (see page 225) that she executed with comparable skill and artistry.*

161

THE COMIC BOOK IN MOLA ART • *Lurid picture stories featuring daredevil exploits and ever-victorious endings are addictive to Cuna boys. Their mothers, in the best pop art tradition, appropriate whole pages showing heroic figures struggling through the most bizarre physical encounters. In an episode which must have delighted the monster-oriented minds of Cuna readers, an enormous hormiga, or ant, holds the invincible Superman in its crusty clutches. An early 1960s comic book cover inspired the torture chamber scene at lower right. In a story called "The Web of the Spinner," El Hombre Murcielago, or Batman, accompanied by his erstwhile sidekick, Robin, rushes to a last-minute rescue of Batwoman, just seconds before the villainous robot pulls a lethal lever. Homage to Walt Disney is paid in this "Hug of War" illustration from a TRUE LIFE ADVENTURES publication which shows grinning starfish tugging to extract dinner from two very reluctant seashells.*

SUPERMAN

162 WALT DISNEY MOTIF

BATMAN

LEGENDS FOR FOLLOWING PAGE:

"THE LITTLE RED HEN" • *The moralistic tale of the hard-working Little Red Hen and her three shiftless companions, the dog, the cat, and the mouse, is known to children in many lands. In this mola a very modern Little Red Hen (La Gallinita Roja) is preparing to cook a delicious cake on an electric hot plate. Throughout her labors of planting, tending, harvesting, and baking, her lazy friends have refused to help, so, as a punitive object lesson to them, she eats the entire cake as they hungrily look on. It is a story that naturally appeals to Cuna mothers, for in San Blas children are constantly being taught industriousness, virtuous conduct, and the principles of right and wrong through daily instruction and traditional chants of* kantules. *On the reverse side (not shown) the game little hen is shown mixing her cake batter.*

ANIMAL KINGDOM COURTROOM SCENE • *Cunas derive their mola designs from many sources, but children's book illustrations remain among their favorites. They lavish unusual care and labor on especially interesting patterns. This amusing pictorial panel shows an animal kingdom courtroom scene. A lordly lion presides as judge while a buzzard acts as scribe and a foxy lawyer pleads his client's case. Two husky policemen have the culprit handcuffed between them and a jury of his peers sits soberly in the background.*

SEWING CAT AND MICE • *The specific tale suggested here is vaguely familiar but remains frustratingly elusive. No doubt, this mola is based on a children's book illustration. A motherly cat is shown contentedly mending, her sewing table at her side, while two strangely bewhiskered mice or rats either bedevil her or keep her company. Rodents, especially rats, are all too common on the San Blas Islands and are impossible to keep out of the loosely constructed bamboo huts with their palm-thatch roofs.*

PUSS-IN-BOOTS • *The celebrated Puss-in-Boots character has traveled to San Blas by way of children's book illustrations and clever advertising. This feline Lothario, far removed from Charles Perrault's fairy tale, seems to be offering his paramour an expensive ladies' wrist watch but there is no telling what his magnanimous gesture signifies.*

least one island, Ailigandi, boasts a library with well-thumbed medical books and other pictorial matter.

As soon as it has been sewn onto a blouse and worn, a mola becomes a design source of its own and for all practical purposes the original is discarded. The sight of a Cuna woman copying directly from an illustration is rare. Some mola-makers are covetous of their designs and are reluctant to discuss where they come from. Molas can be clearly labeled "Tarzan," "Superman," or "Western Horseman," but their sources seem to be generally kept out of sight. Aesthetically it is important to realize that molas inspired by printed matter are interpretations and not merely copies. Such work can show as much flair and imagination as the designs of a more indigenous nature. The amazing thing is that almost any Cuna woman can take a few pieces of mass-produced cotton cloth and turn them into an image so original and beautifully worked that it can make one exclaim in wonder.

What fun it would be if Mark Twain, Hugh Lofting, Edgar Rice Burroughs, Walt Disney, or all those other authors whose characters have been stitched onto molas,

"THE LITTLE RED HEN"

ANIMAL KINGDOM COURTROOM SCENE

SEWING CAT AND MICE

"PUSS IN BOOTS"

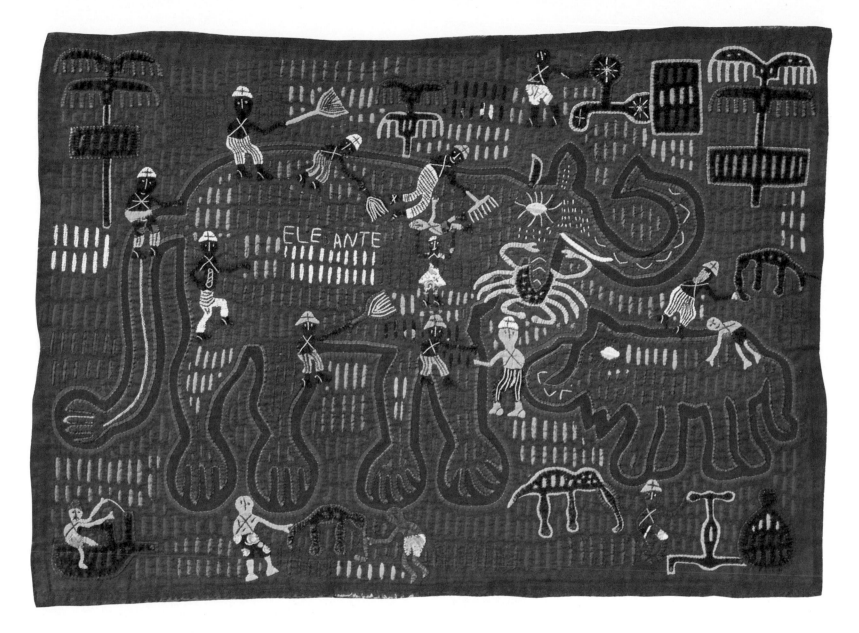

THE ELEPHANT'S BATH • *The very idea of scrubbing down a gigantic pachyderm must have tickled the fancy of this mola-maker, for she lavished a wealth of humorous detail on its elaboration. The pictorial inspiration for this textile is obscure, but it seems reasonable to suppose it came from a children's book illustration. A docile elephant with tiny tusks and a trunk-sized tail is receiving the lavatory ministrations of half a dozen industrious attendants wielding brooms and wearing pith helmets while its offspring stands* *obediently by, possibly waiting its turn. The rest of the scene is one of ultimate confusion—helpers manipulating water taps, a woman hoisting a man over her head, a huge ocean crab clinging to the elephant's chin, and various people involved with various strange-looking creatures. There is a strong circus feeling here, but it can't really be defined until the mola's actual source is discovered. In the meantime it must remain a rare example of consummate needlecraft and a wildly mysterious delight.*

165

could glimpse what marvelous and unexpected textile treasures inspired by their works have come from this chain of isolated islands, all so tiny that on most maps they literally do not exist.

As more books and magazines illustrated by far-out contemporary artists reach the San Blas Islands, it will be interesting to observe how Cunas will react to these exciting graphic images and how the strange designs and colors will influence mola-makers.

MARTINA SWEEPING HER PATIO

ILLUSTRATION FROM "PEREZ AND MARTINA"

RAT AND COCKROACH MOLA

ILLUSTRATION FROM "PEREZ AND MARTINA"

A CHILDREN'S FOLKTALE • *These two molas illustrate the popular Puerto Rican folktale, "Perez and Martina," the story of a refined Spanish cockroach, Martina, who falls in love with a gallant little mouse, Perez. For a Christmas treat Martina concocts a special almond, rice, and raisin dish for Perez, puts it on the fire to cook, and goes outside to sweep her patio. Her paramour smells the delicious mixture cooking, and leaning over to taste it, falls into the pit and dies.*

The scene on one mola shows Martina having just found a rusty coin while working outside her charming tile-roofed dwelling; a nondescript Perez and cooking pot are plainly visible through an open window. It
is captioned La Cucurachita Martina, *"The Little Cockroach, Martina."*

In the second version, Perez is overbalanced and about to topple into a piping hot cauldron resting on a typical Cuna earthenware brazier, and Martina is busily sweeping her patio. The title has been localized to read "The Cockroach, Mandinga, and the Mouse, Perez," presenting a clever play on words since the mola came from an island called Mandinga. The book, written in 1932 by Pura Belpré and illustrated by Carlos Sanchez, is adapted from a folktale and has long been a children's favorite throughout Spanish-speaking countries.

167

DETAIL FROM ROMULUS AND REMUS

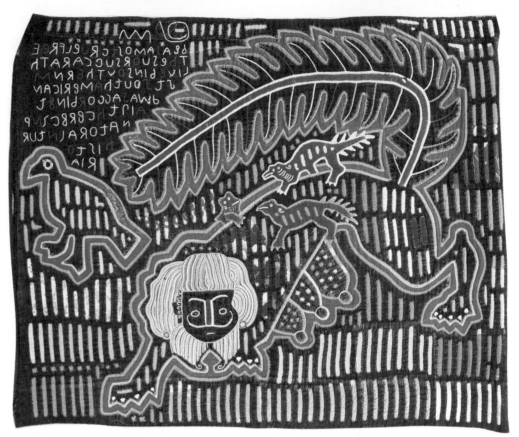

THE SU OR SUCCARATH

CAMEL AND RIDERS

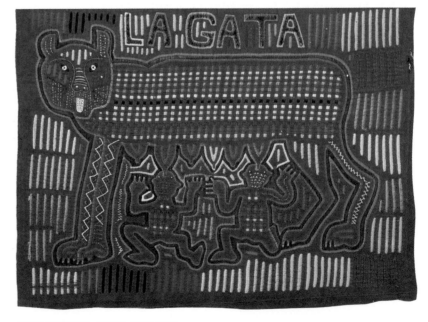

ROMULUS AND REMUS

168

THE MYTHICAL SU • *Although the reverse lettering is jumbled almost beyond deciphering, this fabulous beast is identified, as nearly as can be made out, as a Su, or Succarath. The embroidered legend further reads that, "according to a 17th century natural history, the Succarath lived in southernmost South America," and described it as "most cruel and fierce." As in so many instances, the mola's reverse side carries an almost identical design. Could the name of this human-faced creature, Succarath, be a corruption of Succubus, that evil female demon from the pages of antiquity which ensnares men with her lust? At least part of the answer can be discovered in the whimsical woodcut below.*

CAMEL AND RIDERS • *This Arabian setting suggests exotic lands far beyond the horizons of San Blas. A desert tribesman serenades his fair harem beauty as they travel aboard the proverbial "ship of the desert," in this case a caparisoned but sadly discombobulated dromedary. Although the lumbering beast's features are distinctly cameloid, the mola-maker puzzled over them and finally decided to call the animal caballo, or horse, instead of a camelo. The provocative female figure in the lower right-hand corner is hopefully meant to portray a belly dancer.*

ROMULUS AND REMUS • *The story of Romulus, founder of Rome, and his twin brother, Remus, is known to almost every schoolchild. Born of a union between Mars and a vestal virgin, they were abandoned as infants, left to die, found and nurtured by a she-wolf. When a picture postcard of the statue commemorating that seminal event fell into Cuna hands it was immediately transformed into a delightful mola. The woman who stitched it was faithful to beast and suckling babes in her reproduction but she was unfamiliar with either wolves or the legend, so she labeled her animal what she believed it to be: La Gata, "The Cat."*

WOODCUT OF THE SU-MONSTER • *Research for the Su, or Succarath, leads one to an early bestiary,* André Thevet's Singularités de la France Antarctique Autrement nommé Amérique, *published in Antwerp by Christopher Plantin in the year 1558. One of the plates depicts a fanciful representation of the Su-monster. A later drawing, obviously copied from this, the original, somehow found its way to the San Blas Islands and served as a model for this unusual mola.*

STATUE OF ROMULUS AND REMUS • *This famous Etruscan statue of Romulus and Remus provided the image for the mola on the preceding page. Carved in the fourth or fifth century* B.C., *it is one of the most reproduced figures in the world. The idea of children being suckled by an animal would naturally appeal to the Cuna's mythical sensibility.*

PHOTOGRAPHS OF CUNA LIFE

CUNA BOY AT WINDOW

It is believed that sometime in the remote past the great god, Ibeorgun, instructed the Cuna people in ceremonies, customs, medicines, ways of dress, and morality. He also decreed a division of labor. A man's work consists of cultivating food, hunting, fishing, gathering coconuts and firewood, building and repairing the hut, weaving baskets, making his own and his sons' clothing, carving wooden implements and utensils, and keeping the boat in good order. A woman takes care of the children, keeps the house clean and the fires burning, fetches fresh water, prepares food, unloads the boats, and sews female garments, most specifically the mola blouse.

To this day Cuna village life follows this predetermined pattern. The working day's rhythm allows plenty of time for relaxing with friends and family. Needs are easily met, and within this tightly knit structure the independent Cuna spirit is free to soar.

Those persons primarily interested in mola art might easily overlook the more mundane aspects of San Blas Island life until it dawns on them that virtually every Cuna activity has been portrayed in graphic detail on their brightly appliquéd blouses.

HEADMAN AND WIFE,
RIO SIDRA

HULLING RICE • *Rice is a staple in the Cuna diet. It is harvested on the mainland, tied into sheaves, and brought to the villages where it is hulled and winnowed by the women. The tough brittle grains are placed in huge mortars and vigorously pounded by using alternating strokes with heavy wooden pestles.*

RICE, HULLED AND IN SHEAVES

HULLING RICE WITH MORTAR
AND PESTLES

BASKETMAKING • *Basketmaking is a man's job and is usually done in spare moments. Reeds are gathered on the mainland and separated into thin layers in preparation for weaving. Besides producing both plain and patterned fire fans, these reed weavers turn out skillfully made baskets in a variety of shapes and sizes. Containers for storing grain are large and tightly woven, whereas sewing baskets are smaller and of a medium weave (page 5). Large loosely constructed buskets like the one shown here are used for transporting fruits, coconuts, and other produce.*

173

CAYUCO UNDER SAIL • *With sails looking as though they could use some concentrated appliqué work, this family trio can still head for their mainland plantation at a much better clip than paddling. Cayucos are the essential key to Cuna island life and are used by both men and women. The little boy on the next page has already learned to manage a miniature cayuco without adult supervision. Children lead independent lives on these carefree islands, and it is not unusual to see a child quite some distance from shore paddling his own canoe. The large fish being scaled with a* machete *was one of several caught that day. Prized as a delicacy, it is found in abundance for only a week or two out of each year.*

CUNA MAN SCALING FISH
WITH MACHETE

SMALL BOY PLAYING IN *CAYUCO*

175

MEDICINE MAN
WITH *UCHU*

THERAPEUTIC MEDICINE DOLLS • *Families have collections of therapeutic idols that are kept in boxes ready for use if illness strikes. When called to duty, this box and contents will be placed beside the hammock of the sick person. The medicine man will be summoned to sing, give medicinal potents, and place an incense pot filled with smoking cocoa beans underneath the hammock. As modern medicine is being introduced to the islands, some Indians rely less on the old cures, whereas others still reject modern ways. Many, however, will use both to doubly ensure results.*

YOUNG GIRL WITH
GOLD NECKLACE

CUNA GRAVES • *Two gracefully smoothed burial plots are pictured here with bowls, mugs, and incense pot belonging to the deceased placed reverently on top of the red clay mound. The wooden posts at either end of the grave extend downwards into the burial pit where the dead man, wrapped in his hammock, is suspended between them. The grave marker is lettered on its far side with the name of the deceased, the island he came from, and the date and time of his death. It is traditional among Cunas never to mention the name of a person once he or she has died. The mola,* CUNA BURIAL, *on page 73 describes in fine stitchery another version of this subject.*

PORTRAIT OF A CUNA MATRIARCH

FENCE OF CARVED WOODEN FIGURES • *Indian life throughout Central and South America has been distilled into a fine blend of indigenous and imposed cultures. The two have maintained a tacit idols-behind-altars coexistence for centuries. Some Cunas have been converted to the teachings of Christ, but at the same time ambivalently retained faith in the powers of their traditional gods.*

FOUR PORTRAITS OF CUNA MEN

MOLA BLOUSE WITH BRASSIERES • *Some progressive-minded Cunas, particularly those who spend time in Panama, have adopted western-style fashions in women's wear. The brassiere, which is as alien to San Blas as it is to most primitive societies, must have titillated the sly humor of mola-makers for, once the idea was introduced, it suddenly began to appear as an artistic design stitched across the fronts of blouses. Within a few months the pattern had caught on and was showing up throughout the one-hundred-and-some-odd-mile stretch of islands.*

WESTERN CLOTHING & COMMON OBJECTS

Generally, in the acculturation process between European and primitive societies, menfolk are the first to adopt western-style clothing. So it is among the Cunas of San Blas. While most women cling to their native costume, the men, partly because of their prolonged exposure to outside ways, now dress in the white man's manner.

Since their first contact with Europeans more than four and a half centuries ago, Cuna men have been going abroad as sailors on pirate boats, Yankee trading ships, whalers, and, more recently, merchant vessels. Great numbers of them also work in the Canal Zone and have become accustomed to wearing the same dress as their employers.

Nonetheless, some of the men in San Blas, particularly those older ones of authority, still sew their own shirts, using a distinctive pattern handed down for generations, a style reminiscent of loose-fitting 19th-century American work smocks. For most, however, it seems easier, since the introduction of factory-made clothing, to simply purchase a shirt or other garments as needed.

Cuna women, who are entrusted with home and family,

ELECTRIC FANS • *Electric fans, always welcome in tropical lands, were suddenly the rage among mola-makers in 1974. In this design they have become twin pansies or anthropomorphic figures. Even the most worldly traveler might do a double take when a comely young Cuna approaches wearing this motif, with the circulating blades of the fans appearing to strike her at exactly breast height.*

187

CLOTHING STYLES, OLD AND NEW

• Customs are changing in San Blas and prejudices against western-style clothing are beginning to break down. On at least two islands the women no longer wear molas. These changing attitudes are best observed in the dress of school-age girls, many of whom now wear dresses. The young mother pictured here, with modern diaper pins stuck in her blouse, has retained her traditional Cuna costume, but her baby is swaddled in the latest commercial infant's wear. Some girl children may later return to wearing molas, but once manufactured clothing has been generally accepted it can be only a matter of time before the mola blouse ceases to be worn except at tribal functions by a few tradition-bound women.

seldom leave the islands and have become the conservators of tribal customs. Throughout San Blas, with the peculiar exception of two comparatively modernized islands, they have managed to keep their traditional costume intact and, with the current commercial interest in molas, have made it an important part of their economy.

During the past few years mola-makers have taken a fancy to portraying western-style clothing on their mola panels. One reason for this might be that Cuna men, returning from mainland cities with their purchases, have been bringing home more and more machine-made clothing for themselves and their children. A woman, otherwise totally garbed in traditional dress, can share the "modern look" by appliquéing it onto her blouse. But more probably her choice can be credited to the great Cuna delight in portraying something new and different on a blouse. Whatever the reason, the results are eye-catching and often charged with subtle wit and humor.

Considering this, it is not out of character to see several women on an island proudly wearing blouses with spectacular images of frilly dresses, men's skivvy shirts, or even a baby's romper suit emblazoned across them. An even more incongruous sight is that of a barefoot Indian woman with a pair of high-fashion shoes stitched onto the front and back panels of her blouse. The startling appearance of shirts, trousers, neckties, bathing trunks, and ladies' underwear as mola designs makes Cuna women look like walking advertisements for the garment industry. One year's fad was the flowery brassiere design, sewn as a double image so the top bra could be worn just about where an actual Maidenform should appear.

The first hints of acculturation showed up on turn-of-the-century molas in the form of sailing ships, anchors

TEAPOTS, HANDSAWS, AND MACHETES
• *Contact with traders and the outside world has been responsible for all manner of curious objects turning up in Cuna huts. This ornate teapot and its variformed underlings probably arrived via the pages of a catalog selling household wares. Although Cunas are mostly boiled-in-the-bucket coffee drinkers, such a teapot could very easily be found in a native dwelling.*

Serruchos, or handsaws, are not new to San Blas. This stylized pair, dwarfing the man between them, has left realism far behind; indeed, some examples of this same pattern are so abstract that it is hard to see the saws at all.

Machetes are commonplace among San Blas Indians. Of all a man's meager worldly possessions, perhaps the single most useful item is his machete. These are shown sheathed in their tooled leather scabbards, arranged so as to form a pleasing design.

TEAPOTS

190   HANDSAWS   MACHETES

with chains, umbrellas, and other imported items, but not until more recent times has the depiction of everyday things from the outside world really caught on.

Over the years diligent mola-makers have consistently documented nearly every utilitarian object that has ever come their way. Tools, household utensils, and other implements seem to carry the most appeal. Variations of hammers, saws, pliers, machetes, scissors, and other tools were current in the 1970s. Native items like fire fans, boat paddles, cooking pots, and fishing spears gave way to bird cages, kerosene lanterns, fish lures, food choppers, electric fans, and silverware. The teapot mola illustrated on page 190 seemed unique in 1974 but by now it, too, might have a score of imitators.

One wonders what new objects will inspire the blouses of future seasons. Could 1977 be the year of the cement mixer, the Polaroid camera, or perhaps the chain saw? Might not a new fad be the bristling and irresistible shape of an exploded multipurpose Swiss Red Cross knife like those so prominently displayed in Panama's duty-free shop windows?

There is no speculating for only time can tell. Cuna women are always on the lookout for new designs, and sometimes the most unexpected commonplace object will be converted into a thing of beauty. Each mola is a small celebration of some passing fancy and even the maker can't name the subject of her next creation. One must keep in mind that it is the quality of the artist's imagination and skillful needlework that elevate a piece of Cuna stitchery to the status of art.

MACHETE • *The heavy steel blade of this* machete *serves the Indians as an everyday cutting and digging tool, as well as a fearful weapon. The scrolls and fancy tooling on leather scabbards inspire the flowery* machete *designs pictured on molas.*

TROUSERS • *In this age of woman's lib, one might suspect that the wife who stitched this pair of* pantalones, *or trousers—complete with stylish patch pockets and outside buttons—onto her blouse may have been trying to get a message across to her husband.*

PARTY DRESS • *In Panama this little girl's puff-sleeved party dress would have been worn only on special occasions, but in San Blas it became the design for a blouse used for everyday wear.*

BABY'S ROMPER SUIT • *Inside Cuna huts one frequently sees long rows of modern infant's wear carefully arranged on plastic hangers suspended from roof beams. Fathers returning*

from the mainland bring back an amazing array of the petite doll-like clothing commonly sold in stores and stalls along city streets. This fleecy romper suit, manufactured abroad, carries a mother's loving touch: the word BEBE, *or baby, embroidered where a label would ordinarily have been.*

PAIR OF SHOES • *San Blas islanders usually go barefoot, as the clean-swept paths, earthen floors, and sandy beaches encourage it. However, fashions change, and more and more foreign-made shoes are being brought home by men who work in the Canal Zone or journey to the cities on business. Mola-makers soon made shoes one of the more amusing motifs for their blouses. It is wildly incongruous to see a barefoot Indian wearing a mola depicting shoes.*

FOLDED SHIRTS • *The woman who made this mola was inspired by her husband's ready-made shirt which arrived folded and pinned to the manufacturer's stiff cardboard. To leave no doubt in anybody's mind she spelled out on cuffs and pockets the word "shirt" in disorganized Spanish—I-S-A-M-A-C—*Camisa.

DECORATED T-SHIRT • *T-shirts came to San Blas via the Canal Zone during World War II and nearly all males wear them now. Lately, decorated T-shirts have come into fashion. This one shows a happy musician with congo drums and maracas.*

TROUSERS

PARTY DRESS

BABY'S ROMPER SUIT

PAIR OF SHOES

MARIACHI SINGER WITH ROOSTER • *Jorge Negrete was one of Mexico's greatest singers of ranch-type ballads. Here he is seen wearing the typical costume of a mariachi singer from Guadalajara, his lavishly embroidered sombrero thrown back on his head. The finely plumed rooster he is holding may symbolize the inspiration for a hit song called "El Gallo" (The Rooster). The introduction of guitar-strumming Elvis Presley complemented by a wildly gyrating figure conforms to young Cunas' interest in rock-and-roll music heard mainly over transistor radios. Two unrelated record album covers must have supplied the elements for this delightful mola.*

GAMES & ENTERTAIN-MENTS

L ife in the San Blas Islands is easy by any standard. The tropical climate is mild and there is always a soft sea breeze sweeping the offshore islands. Food can be had for the gathering; the sea abounds with fish and the jungle provides a variety of game, fruits, and vegetables, both wild and cultivated on tiny plantations. After the daily chores, which consist mainly of paddling to the mainland for fresh water, doing laundry, gathering firewood, and tending crops, there is plenty of leisure time to be enjoyed by all. But Cunas are not inclined toward idleness. The men weave baskets, carve wooden figures (*Uchus*), or work on their boats. The women make molas, whole groups of them sitting together, talking and sewing, often by lantern light far into the night.

For everyday entertainment there are the usual sports and numerous children's games. Community diversion includes ball games, ceremonial dances, and *chicha* festivals. Music is always welcome. Reed flutes are traditional Cuna instruments, but some of the younger men play guitars. A few families have transistor radios which fill the air with Latin-American rhythms in noisy competition with the Canal Zone station's current pop hits from the U.S. An occasional windup phonograph with a dusty stack

DETAIL OF ELVIS PRESLEY

195

BABY'S
RATTLE
BLOUSE

BABY'S
PLASTIC
RATTLE

BABY'S PLASTIC RATTLE MOTIF • *On the blouse above, a common toy has been transformed into an exquisite work of art. The figure's doll-like features have been elaborated upon while the nursery rhyme cow has become a horse jumping over the moon. Contrary to speculation of those seeking symbolic meaning in every mola, the smaller images are not shadowy soul figures but graphic repeats.*

The actual toy, a baby's plastic rattle imported from Hong Kong, was found in a Cuna hut. Although cast aside, it inspired the charming anthropomorphic shapes seen on this page.

This mola-maker's fancy took a more humorous turn for her back panel. Eyeglasses and toothy smiles were worked in, rows of buttons became neckties, and, while the moon disappeared, the animal changed into a man-faced beast with flying mane and three tails. Except for the two gnome-like creatures which have taken up guardian positions, this variation appears gay and light-hearted.

196

VARIATION OF BABY'S RATTLE MOTIF

MEXICAN RECORD ALBUM DESIGN • *Mexican music is popular throughout Central America and can be had in great variety from Panama City's many record shops. Antonio Aguilar is famous as a movie actor and a singer of lively ranch-type songs. Here he is pictured standing beside his horse, elegantly garbed in the charro costume and wide-brimmed, embroidered sombrero traditionally worn by mariachi singers. This picture was no doubt copied from a record album cover which turned up in one of the larger San Blas Islands supplied with enough electricity to operate a record player.*

TWO DESIGNS FROM RECORD ALBUM COVERS • *These are the front and back panels of the same blouse featuring on one side a musical group called "The Originals," who play a duet on their guitars as they cast sidelong glances at one another. On the reverse side two oddly costumed figures pose together under the legendary name, Pedro Infante, a singer who rose to fame during the 1940s as one of Mexico's most popular stars of stage and screen. It is probable that both molas were inspired by record album covers brought to San Blas from Panama.*

MEXICAN MOVIE POSTER • *This flamboyant panel is a prime example of what a pictorial mola can be. The title reads, "La Novia del Torero," or "The Bullfighter's Sweetheart," and was copied from an illustration, perhaps a circular or a movie poster or a record album cover. A torero in his traditional "suit of lights," the dazzling, gold-thread embroidered costume worn by successful artists of the cape and sword, is preparing for another life-or-death contest in the bullring. In this dramatic scene he and his betrothed solemnly clasp hands in a sacred vow before the Virgin of Guadalupe, who looks on in glorious approval. Lola Beltran, the star whose name is displayed above, is now in retirement, but during her heyday she reigned supreme as Mexico's all-time great in the singing of popular ranch-type songs.*

of antiquated 78-rpm records can still be found, and on islands with power from electric generators there will be at least one modern record player. Recordings are purchased on the mainland, most of them imported from the U.S. or Mexico, and album covers become subjects for mola panels.

Playing cards, not commonly used by Cunas, show up in the islands where the flashy face cards and jokers inspire medieval-looking blouses. Kings, queens, and especially jacks, glorified further by repetition, join the great mola parade. The jokers, playful by definition, are found singly, doubled, quadrupled, and even as substitutes for another outsider, Santa Claus (page 202). Occasionally a mola will show four piles of dealt cards with the players' hands reaching for them.

Besides customary land and water activities Cunas enjoy many thought-provoking contests. There is more than a passing interest in board games such as checkers, Parcheesi (page 202), and chess. These and other games like dominoes are played by young men and boys who set up little tables in the shade and while away long hot afternoons. Boys also shoot marbles on the hard-packed sand.

BOY WITH BATMAN KITE • *The same offshore breezes that keep the San Blas Islands free of insect pests are ideal for flying kites. Fathers returning from the mainland often bring cheap plastic or paper kites as gifts for their sons, and are not opposed to joining in the fun. This little boy was working on a Batman kite which, unfortunately, proved more decorative than airworthy.*

ANTHROPOMORPHIC KITES • *Each season seems to produce its favorite mola motifs, and on some islands 1975 was the time when the kite-flying craze in San Blas inspired a kite mola craze. Anthropomorphic kites vied for popularity with fancy bras (page 186) and electric fans (page 187) as modish new designs. The shoe and dress motifs (page 193) of the previous year had already become passé and were rarely sewn although they were still being worn.*

TV SHOW, "THE FLINTSTONES" • *Cunas visiting the mainland are enraptured by television. A reminder of the popular caveman cartoon series, "The Flintstones" (Ospica Piedras) was carried home to San Blas in the form of a TV program announcement. The Spanish translates—The Flintstones. Channel 2, Friday, at 7:30 P.M. The scene is enclosed in a frame suggesting the screen of a TV set. Fred and Barney, the main characters, seated in a boat, have encountered what seems to be a walrus. The frantic figure in the center is probably the station's announcer.*

BOY WITH BATMAN KITE

MEXICAN MOVIE POSTER

ANTHROPOMORPHIC KITES

TV SHOW: "THE FLINTSTONES"

DR. DOLITTLE BLOUSE • *The eccentric Dr. Dolittle, his parrot companion, Polynesia, contentedly perched on his top hat, is portrayed here leaning on the fabulous two-headed "pushmi-pullya" created by Hugh Lofting in his classic, The Story of Dr. Dolittle. Since costumes and adornment closely approximate those of the 1967 Twentieth Century-Fox* *movie starring Rex Harrison as Dr. Dolittle, this mola was probably inspired by publicity for the film. The Doctor's FREE CASH CARNIVAL is advertised in bold letters, and together the banners read: "Get .50¢, $1.00, $1.50, or $2.00 in cash for Doctor Dolittle ('s) proof of purchase seals."*

201

PARCHEESI BOARD • *Board games such as checkers, chess, and backgammon, which have managed to find their way to some of the world's most remote and primitive outposts, are also frequently seen in San Blas. This Parcheesi board has all the clean-cut*

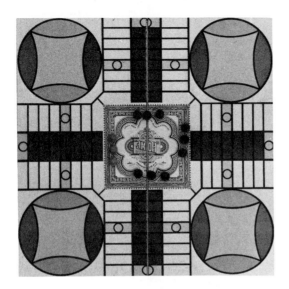

BOARD GAME MOLA

lines of modern design but none of the naïve charm produced by the Cuna artist who copied an earlier model for her mola.

BOARD GAME MOLA • *This mola-maker's careful representation of a Parcheesi board shows players as well as pieces. The game, which originated in India, is played the world over. A U.S. toy company, Selchow and Righter, has manufactured Parcheesi sets for over 100 years, perhaps even the one with instructions in Spanish used as a pattern for the mola shown here.*

JOKERS • *These jocular refugees from a deck of battered playing cards could hardly be resisted by the woman who chose them to decorate her blouse. The jesters' belled caps and jolly features must have reminded her of Christmas because she confused their personalities and tacked on a "Santa Claus" label stitched in topsy-turvy lettering.*

Kites, flown when the wind is right, show up on molas with embroidered faces (page 200). Girls play hopscotch or swing golden-haired, blue-eyed dolls in miniature hammocks while drowsy babies fondle gourd rattles and cheap plastic toys (page 196).

It is on the mainland, however, that the best ideas for molas based on the entertainment theme are born. Window-shopping is a game in itself, and Cuna men are often seen escorting traditionally clad wives, sisters, or family groups through the crowded streets of Panama City and Colón. The women seem not to miss a thing, and some of their impressions will later be introduced into fine molas.

Some designs based on movie advertisements (page 201) and record album covers (pages 194 and 195) must have been copied from actual printed sources, but the initial incentive to use such graphic images may often have been the result of an exciting mainland visit.

Carnivals and circuses, always big attractions throughout Latin America, have all the visual elements needed for inspired mola-making, and the opportunity is not lost on Cuna women. Clowns are frequently depicted on molas, as are menageries of strange animals. Less common circus scenes show aerialists (page 204), jugglers, and the all-time winner, a complete panorama of the big top (page 205), showing multiple action in the center ring.

LEGENDS FOR FOLLOWING PAGE:

WEIGHT-GUESSING GAME • *In this curious mola a buxom woman in urban dress operates a spring scale much like those used in carnival weight-guessing games. The figure suspended in the chair looks more like a monkey or a disgruntled cat than it does a man. Some of the lettering alongside the scale's support post reads "82 pounds and three ounces." This mola may, indeed, have been inspired by a weight-guessing game, but more than likely its source was a book illustration or an advertisement of some kind. Mola sources are sometimes lost with the passage of time, and trying to recover them can be a tedious and frustrating endeavor.*

JACK OF SPADES • *Card playing is not common among Cuna Indians. However, cards do turn up in the San Blas Islands and mola-makers, always quick to respond to new and different visual challenges, take delight in using them—especially the flamboyant face cards—as designs for their blouses. In this case a Jack of Spades is rendered into stitchery with appealing fidelity in spite of the spade suit's conversion from black to red.*

CIRCUS AERIALISTS • *The trapeze artistry of these circus aerialists is matched by the sewing artistry of the Cuna woman who made this mola. As they make contact high up in the lofty confines of the star-spangled tent where their performance has begun, one senses what is perhaps a tragedy in the making, for the man, as catcher, has grasped his female partner's wrists but she refuses to release her fly bar. And, even if she did, without his legs wrapped around the canvas-covered ropes of his own trapeze, he could not support her weight once they were locked together.*

WEIGHT-GUESSING GAME

JACK OF SPADES

CIRCUS AERIALISTS

CIRCUS EXTRAVAGANZA • *Circuses and carnivals are time-honored diversions in Latin American countries. In the course of a year several traveling shows might come to Panama, and Cunas visiting the mainland would be sure to attend them. As exotic in their own way as the performers they are watching, Cuna families help to make up an audience completely entranced by the unusual sights and sounds of the Big Top. Given the mola-maker's flare for reproducing spectacular events in stitchery, it would be strange, indeed, if such visual bombardments did not inspire fresh designs. As the result of these man-and-trained-animal performances, circus themes are frequently found sewn onto molas. This crowded, single-ring arena features clown and acrobatic acts, as well as a trapeze artist suspended from a hot-air balloon and a banjo-plucking troubadour perched precariously on a horse which nonchalantly munches flowers. While one gangling clown paints spots on the troubadour's horse, a dwarf is about to precipitate a terrible tumble of confidently balanced acrobats by poking a stick into the already battered spokes of the unicycle's wheel.* 205

DATED POLITICAL CAMPAIGN MOLA • *Somehow the propagandistic edge is taken off this political message when it is translated from a gaudy campaign poster into a finely worked blouse panel. It was no doubt unintentional, but the V for Victory pattern repeated across the top border complements the words "Symbol of Triumph." The date, 1952, refers* to *that particular campaign year, establishes the mola's age, and confirms a certain quality of workmanship which was in vogue a quarter of a century ago. Flags, bovine portrait, and party slogans have all been combined to make this mola an appliquéd monument to the CPN organization.*

THE POLITICAL SCENE

Cunas have the ballot in Panama's national elections and since they are encouraged to back certain candidates, their unified vote can be influential. To win this bloc, party propaganda is widely distributed in the islands and delegates sometimes visit the territory. This has led quite naturally to the use of political imagery on molas.

Nearly all political molas fall into three main categories—those that show one or more candidates; those that show elaborate party symbols; and a small percentage that are satirical commentaries. Insignia seem to have been introduced first, probably in the 1940s, whereas most molas showing party leaders date from the late 1950s to the present. Sometimes Cuna blouses will portray an office-seeker on one side and his party's symbol on the other. Examples of the rare satirical molas are generally based on newspaper cartoons or propaganda sheets and are, more often than not, beautiful creations of complex stitchery.

Molas with political motifs are usually produced shortly before or immediately following elections. Many are snapped up by collectors as soon as the women are willing to sell them, and a few may even end up in the possession of party functionaries as campaign souvenirs. As with many inscribed molas the lettering gets jumbled so that

DETAIL OF GALINDO PORTRAIT

207

PANAMANIAN PARTY POLITICAL INSIGNIA • *The Panamanian party's slogan ''For a Better Panama'' promises a new day for the nation by showing this lushly endowed landscape with a contented worker warmed by the rays of a glorious rising sun. The reverse side of this mola is the political triumvirate on page 209.*

CARRIZO POLITICAL POSTER & REPUBLICAN PARTY INSIGNIA • *These two designs comprise the front and back panels of the same blouse. The front side shows a carefully worked portrait, party flags, insignia, pointing hands, and an abundance of descriptive information on the candidate, Dr. Maximo Carrizo, who can also be seen in a more naïve portrait on page 114. The lettering states that he is running for the congress in Colón on the Republican party ticket symbolized by a deer's head, for the period 1964–1968. Above the flags is inscribed* NELE CARRIZO. Nele *in Cuna dialect means a headman.*

The blouse's reverse side displays the Republican party emblem and states that one should ''vote with the deer'' as it is La insignia del triunfo, *''The sign of victory.'' The names Koenono and Bazan are probably those of running mates.*

PANAMANIAN POLITICAL PARTY INSIGNIA

CARRIZO POLITICAL POSTER

REPUBLICAN PARTY INSIGNIA

208

POLITICAL TRIUMVIRATE • Cuna artists have an unusual talent for capturing the essence of their subjects, although they tend more toward stylization and seldom attempt realistic likenesses when portraying the human form. Realism as such is not of great importance to them, nor does it naturally suit their sewing techniques. The maker of this excellent triple portrait not only displays her skill for precise needlework but also consciously attempts, and succeeds in creating, three distinct personalities. Noses, chins, hairlines, as well as the shape and tilt of each man's head have all been carefully studied. Accompanying the bespectacled Dr. Arnulfo Arias are two of his political cohorts, probably Lawyer Luis Garcia Deparedes and Engineer Celso Carbonell.

POLITICAL ORATOR • *The backwards-jumbled lettering on this political mola reads in part, "Popular reelection, Chiari, Coytiau, CPN insignia" and includes widely separated numerals forming what appears to be the date 1970. In the center is a very Cuna-looking orator wearing a wristwatch and gesticulating as he holds the carved cane symbolizing his authority. He also has a wonderfully Picassoesque face, which might do more to discourage votes than to attract them. The Cunas' keen interest in politics is frequently extended to molas, where they do not hesitate to satirize the most sacred cows of the political scene. Along the sides party flags and bespectacled, starry-eyed office seekers are arranged in columns above their respective names. A strip of cloth has been sewn onto the mola's right edge to increase its width, a measure which sometimes becomes necessary when a woman loses her trim figure to pregnancy or overeating.*

slogans become hopelessly confused. Candidates whose names contain *s*'s, *n*'s, or *z*'s seem to suffer most in this alphabetic scramble. Panamanian political slogans are endlessly florid and patriotic. Over the years most have glorified a multitude of splinter parties expressing the hopes and aspirations of the common man. The general run of posters and leaflets reaching San Blas show portraits of *politicos* looking their illustrious best. Whenever possible, professional titles—Doctor and Lawyer are the most respected—precede their names, unless, of course, a man is so well known that only his surname needs be announced in bold letters across the banner. Mola-makers seem fascinated by candidates who wear glasses, deliberately distorting their features with extravagant horn-rimmed spectacles.

Gaudy portraits adorning a mola blouse may bear little resemblance to the actual presidential or senatorial choices, but identity is clarified when the party's blatant message is committed to stitchery. Treatment is not always sympathetic, and mola-makers seem to have a way of exposing the very essence of political folly. They find exceedingly humorous the pompous and often bizarre forms it takes and are not immune to some of the more subtle innuendos. For instance, an anti-Arias mola (page 212) portrays this prominent ex-leader as an octopus—a Cuna devil symbol—promoting discrimination and other evils while maintaining a strangulation grip on constitutional law, the Panamanian people, and everything else a public holds sacred during election campaigns. No doubt lifted directly from a propagandistic cartoon, this translation into a brightly colored image seems all the more effective worn on an Indian woman's blouse.

One can never be quite sure whether Cunas take politics

LEGENDS FOR FOLLOWING PAGE:

POLITICAL PROPAGANDA CARTOON
• *Octopi, along with devils and other monstrous creatures which symbolize evil to Cunas, are disdainfully reproduced on molas without fear of retribution. It seems the more awesome the creature, the more likely it is to be used as a blouse design. This terrible looking octopod, with tentacles labeled "discrimination", "foreign trade," and other pertinent campaign issues, is meant to characterize Dr. Arnulfo Arias, ex-president of the Republic of Panama, who was running for reelection. This design was evidently taken from a political cartoon, implications of which are fairly obvious to even politically naïve observers.*

SATIRICAL POLITICAL CARTOON • *The National Liberation Party's candidate, Roberto Chiari, was president of Panama from late 1960 until 1964. This political cartoon is captioned "Chiari Suena Con Los Sapitos," and shows him lying on his couch dreaming about* sapitos, *or little toads. The word* sapo *is derogatory in Panama for it also signifies spy, undercover man, or traitor. The idea of a legion of placard-bearing toads appearing to torment a man in his dreams must have intrigued this mola-maker, who may very well have shared the cartoonist's anti-Chiari views.*

POLLING PLACE • *Four very formal looking gentlemen are seated at a long table under exaggerated CPN party banners. They are the delegated officials who oversee elections and check off registered voters. The ballot box is placed at one end of the table with a ballot inserted partway into its slot. The message on the bottom of the mola states that one should "vote with this flag." Political posters and handbills are usually kept simple, as many voters cannot read or write and must choose by party symbol.*

211

POLITICAL PROPAGANDA CARTOON

SATIRICAL POLITICAL CARTOON

POLLING PLACE

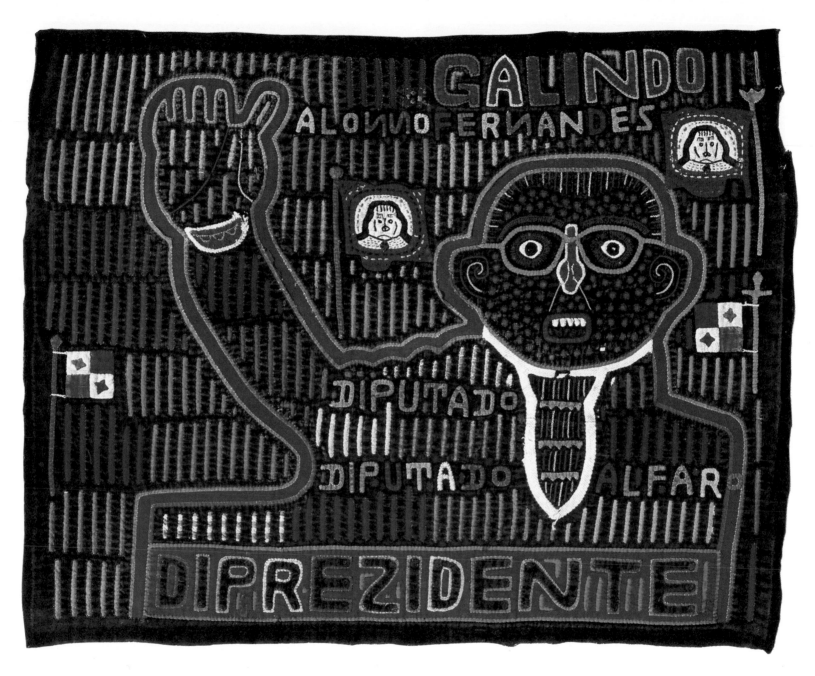

'GALINDO FOR PRESIDENT' POSTER • When Galindo ran for the presidency of Panama, his face became a familiar spectacle throughout the land. His clearly defined visage caught the fancy of several astute mola-makers, and within a matter of weeks it was fashionably adorning new blouses all over San Blas. Although the sudden transformation into a folk art idiom (this being a prime example) had somewhat altered the original, there was no mistaking the man represented—he was essentially the same, still "The Candidate," his features eminently sincere and his arm raised high in a universal gesture signifying strength and leadership.

213

JORGE RAMIREZ

DR. MAXIMO CARRIZO

COL. JOSÉ REMON

ALONSO FERNANDEZ

FOUR POLITICAL PORTRAITS • *The four molas on this page are all variations on a political theme. It is customary for parties to circulate handbills, banners, portrait posters, cartoons, and relevant literature either for their own or against the opposition's candidates. Some of these reach the San Blas Islands and become grist for the mola-maker's mill. In the upper-left-hand corner is Jorge Ramirez, nicknamed Dr.*

214

Fausto by his detractors, who ran for congress on the CPN ticket. Portrayed next is Dr. Maximo Carrizo, who hoped to win the Colón congressional seat. At the lower left is José A. Ramon, who electioneered in the 1952 campaign. The man with the upraised arm is Alonso Fernandez, who ran on the same ticket with presidential candidate Galindo, pictured on the previous page.

seriously or with the proverbial grain of salt. If the caricatures which appear on molas are any indication, it would certainly be the latter. Although active in their own sphere of local government and concerned about decisions on the national level which might affect their well-being, the outside political scene must seem to them like high comedy.

JOHN F. KENNEDY MEMORIAL GLASS • *Drinking glass with JFK Memorial motif typical of those reproduced on various souvenir items immediately following Kennedy's assassination. Printed on the back is the Presidential seal, P.T. boat 109, and the famous rockinc chair, all of which appear on the Kennedy mola on page 217.*

LEGENDS FOR FOLLOWING PAGE:

ANTI-GOLDWATER CARTOON • *Because of close ties but sometimes strained relations between the two countries, Uncle Sam's elections are closely followed by Panamanians. This satirical mola seems to be making an adverse comment on the Republican party's* estrella dilema, *or "star dilemma," Senator Goldwater, who is pictured on the placard hung around the neck of the ukulele-toting, simianlike creature. The dagger grasped in the elephant's trunk suggests there may be nefarious activity afoot in this 1960s campaign. It was probably not without a touch of malicious humor that the mola-maker portrayed this political trio as such an unsavory lot.*

ANTI-CAPITALIST CARTOON • *Gentle floral patterns notwithstanding, this vulturous-looking old bird, with a dollar sign cresting the back of his thronelike chair and horns of plenty decorating his desk, is certainly up to no good as he goes over accounts in his ledger. This design, noteworthy for its fine detail, was probably copied from a political cartoon with anticapitalist sentiments.*

ANTI-COMMUNIST CARTOON • *Anti-Communist propaganda was pervasive in Latin-America long before the advent of Cold-War politics. The 1950s' change of government in Cuba brought about a proliferation of anti-Castro cartoons and posters which continues to this day. Cunas, who are far removed from the actual political arena, find them amusing and reproduce some of the better ones on their mola blouses. This fine example, more subtle than most, represents the revolutionary Castro brothers, Raul and Fidel (so labeled on the peaks of their witch's hats and clearly recognizable by their bearded visages), seasoning a pot of Cuban stew with a generous dose of communism from a bottle with a hammer and sickle on it.* Olla podrida *is a common kind of stew throughout Latin-American countries, but in this instance the Spanish word* podrida *suggests political connotations as it also means putrid or corrupt. The inference is that Dr. Castro is cooking up a rotten mess of stew for the Cuban people, represented by the ailing patient lying abed in the background.*

215

ANTI-COMMUNIST CARTOON

ANTI-CAPITALIST CARTOON

ANTI-GOLDWATER CARTOON

216

JFK MEMORIAL MOLA • *During his years in office President Kennedy enjoyed a wide popularity in Latin-American countries, and even now his memory is held in great esteem by rich and poor alike. His likeness, which had become familiar even in places as remote as San Blas, can still be seen in the form of faded magazine photographs and on souvenir items treasured in native dwellings throughout the Southern Hemisphere. This John F. Kennedy commemorative mola, one of many similar designs that appeared right after his death, shows him gloriously wreathed in laurels and surrounded by the media-touted images associated with his life—the chief of state symbol, his rocking chair, and PT boat 109. This artist, obviously impressed by the famous JFK smile, emphasized it with a double row of teeth more befitting crocodiles than men, especially the illustrious one she meant to revere.*

JACKIE KENNEDY MOLA • *As First Lady of the Land, Jacqueline Kennedy shared much of her husband's immense popularity. Here she is portrayed stylishly dressed, sporting earrings, a fancy purse, and her much-publicized hairdo. Her young daughter, Caroline, appears at her side in a flared party dress. This and the JFK mola pictured above were front and back panels of the same blouse and could have been copied from a pillow cover like those sold in souvenir shops and at post exchanges on most U.S. military bases.*

217

ADVERTISEMENTS, TRADEMARKS, & PACKAGE LABELS

CHIQUITA BANANA • *Cuna mola-makers are also aware that bananas are the tastiest staple of the tropics, and this one paid homage to the lovely fruit by stitching it onto her blouse. Chiquita Banana is known in just about every household that ever popped a cereal box top. Just a hint of that vivacious lady, all decked out in her Carmen Miranda fruit-salad hat and rhumba ruffles, can be seen, but it is enough to convince any confirmed banana eater that she can explode into her catchy song at the slightest sound of a refrigerator door.*

There is a rather widespread misunderstanding currently abroad that molas using advertisements, trademarks, and box or bottle labels as designs are made for tourists only. This misconception should be immediately dispelled by a quick look at a well-rounded mola collection or a pile of older molas in any folk art shop. Advertising molas will show the same obvious signs of wear as other motifs which indicates that the mola-maker intended them for just that purpose—to be worn. The idea of selling molas at all was, until comparatively recent times, only an afterthought. Once a blouse was badly worn or the owner tired of it, it became just a piece of used clothing as far as she was concerned. Molas were made for personal wear, but if an occasional buyer came along, so much the better; the cash was always welcome for stringing into coin necklaces. Of course, the situation has changed radically now that there is a growing demand for molas and some collectors prefer the older designs even if they are somewhat worn and faded.

Tourist molas are easily recognized. They are usually uncomplicated two- or three-layer loosely stitched panels

SOFT DRINK ADVERTISEMENT • *It is sometimes fascinating to compare a mola design with its source, to see how an idea is changed and often greatly improved in its translation from one medium to another. Bottled drinks have become increasingly popular and available on San Blas Islands, where the heat can be parching. It seems natural that the idea of this Hi-Spot gourmand would delight the Cuna mind and sense of humor. When a motif has instant appeal it becomes faddish and can sweep through the islands, copied and recopied dozens of times, always with some slight variation, as was the Hi-Spot mola for a few months in the early 1970s. Such fads usually pass as new designs are introduced and catch on.*

PANAMA CITY BILLBOARD • *This billboard photographed in Panama City in 1973 shows candidly the source for the accompanying mola. The artist's selective eye has eliminated the dreary lettering and six-pack and balanced her design by adding two other drinkers. Canada Dry's Hi-Spot is an effervescent lemon-lime soft drink which really hits the spot in tropical Panama. The billboard claims "Hi-Spot is much more in flavor and in freshness." During the company's nationwide advertising campaign the same advertisement appeared in many newspapers and magazines.*

picturing a single bird, fish, or animal, with a minimum of appliqué work in the background. They show mostly indigenous flora and fauna patterns in bold relief. These are turned out by the thousands and sold in airport stores, boutiques, or museum shops around the world, as well as to tourists visiting the islands. Most are colorful and pleasing to look at, some are nicely designed, others have neat stitching, but they are a far cry from true mola art.

Since they first became known, Cuna molas have been collected and admired for many different reasons, but examples based on the advertising world's pictographic symbols are the ones that have amazed and delighted many of the most sophisticated collectors. The whole idea is like a great spoof of our own mass-production, advertising-oriented society.

This type of imagery may have had its tentative beginnings in the 1930s, but it began to appear more frequently in the 1940s at about the same time that most other acculturation designs started to show up on molas. The wartime prosperity brought about great changes in San Blas Island economy because employment of Cuna men increased dramatically. For the first time this primarily self-sufficient, bartering community had money to spend

SANTA CLAUS • *Even Santa Claus manages to visit the tropics during Christmas celebrations, although he is more likely to arrive in San Blas by plane or* cayuco *(dugout canoe) than by sleigh. Panama City's store windows are lavishly decorated in observance of the holiday spirit, and colorful advertisements appear everywhere. In keeping with the custom, good children receive a bounty of* regalos *(gifts), and Cuna mothers adorn their* molas *with left-over Christmas motifs.*

VERMOUTH ADVERTISEMENT • *In this charming café scene a rather chic couple seated in high-backed chairs enjoy a leisurely apértif. Since the design derives from a liquor advertisement, emphasis has been placed on the product instead of the drinkers and they appear somewhat dwarfed by the clearly labeled bottles of Cinzano. The artist took special care to indicate that the white Vermouth came from France and the red from Italy.*

PANAMA CITY BILLBOARD

SOFT DRINK ADVERTISEMENT

220   SANTA CLAUS

VERMOUTH ADVERTISEMENT

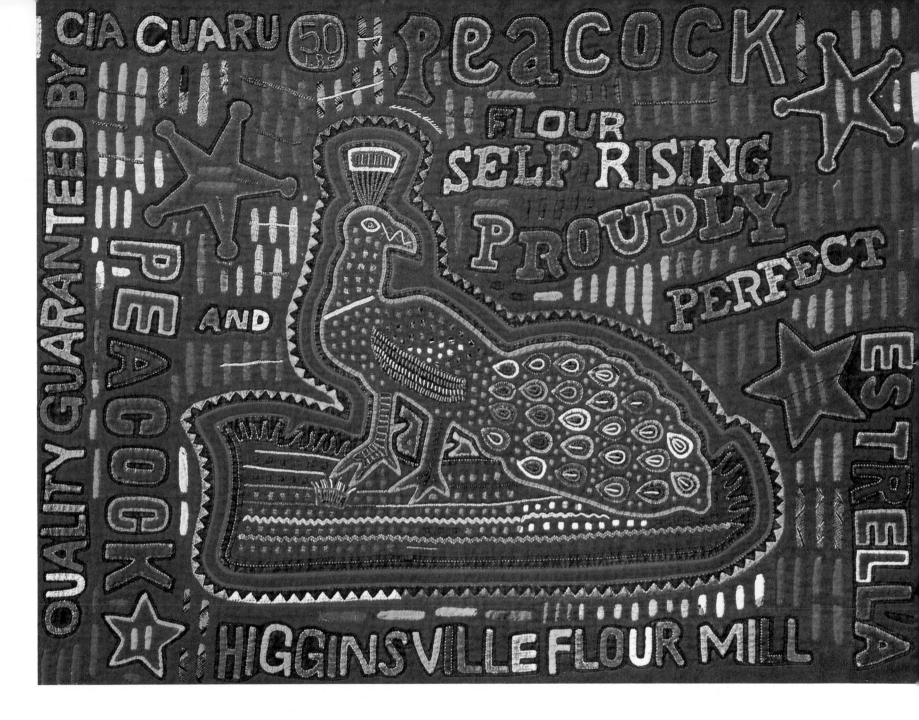

PEACOCK FLOUR SACK • *The Higginsville Flour Mill no longer exists in Higginsville, Missouri, but during the 1940s, when this mola was made, its Peacock brand "proudly perfect, self-rising flour" was exported in colorfully printed cotton sacks that were put to many practical uses by San Blas Islanders. This striking design with its explanatory lettering was worked into a beautiful Cuna blouse and worn with pride to countless festivals before it eventually found a deserved place in a folk art collection. Since Cunas bake their own bread nowadays, commercially made flour has become a common staple in their villages.*

221

NEEDLE, THREAD, AND SCISSORS MOLA • *These twin guardsmen are sewing basket composites with pincushion heads, spools of thread for bodies, scissors for legs, thimbles for helmets, and threaded needles for halberds.*

WOMAN CRUSHING SUGARCANE • *Most of the intoxicating liquor consumed by Cunas is brewed on the islands. Sugarcane is crushed to extract the juice which, when mixed with herbs and corn, will ferment into* chicha, *the alcoholic beverage guzzled during ceremonial gatherings. A primitive but ingenious press has been devised to perform this crushing operation. Shown here is one member of a three-woman team whose job it is to feed the canes into the press, twisting them as they are pushed through in order to extract every drop of liquid. The mildly sweet sticky juice is also drunk and used for cooking in its freshly squeezed state.*

SCOTCH WHISKY BOTTLES • *For a people whose alcoholic drinking habits are generally confined to ceremonial festivals, where they rarely drink commercial varieties, Cuna women are strangely fascinated with the colorful liquor labels that come their way. In this case, a pair of exaggerated screw-top flasks, floating in a sea of stitched crosses, were carefully designed to cover the entire front of a blouse. The wearer of this mola unwittingly became a walking advertisement for "MacLeay Duff's" three-star "Special Mature Cream" Scotch whisky, "Distilled in Scotland" and with a Glasgow imprint.*

RUM ADVERTISEMENT • *This mola with the July, 1949, date appears to be the combination of a liquor advertisement and a political cartoon. The smiling* mono *(monkey) adroitly grasps a wine glass with his prehensile tail while helping himself to one of many bottles displayed as though in a bar. Some of the lettering, like "Ron Nacional Panameno" refers to a native rum, while much of the additional wording seems to be more of a political nature. The word "mono" can mean both monkey and cartoon, so the original could very easily have been a subtle jibe at someone's political opponent. Cunas delight in satirical humor and in picturing animals acting out human roles.*

VODKA ADVERTISEMENT • *The maker of this mola, Enriqueta "Henry" Navarro, from the island of Carti Suitupo, was taken by the Smirnoff vodka advertisement showing a man in a conch shell reaching for a drink—presumably the contents of the bottle pictured in the center. Conch shells are familiar objects along San Blas beaches and are used ritualistically for their sympathetic magic in helping to facilitate childbirth, which may have been why this particular image was chosen for a mola design. Vodka bottles, on the other hand, can turn up almost anywhere. This artist turned the unusual combination to good advantage when she featured it on her mola. The glass at the extreme left has a cherry in it, and the dark form on the bottle, which at first glance looks like an arrowhead, is in reality the company's famed Russian double-eagle trademark.*

CONTEMPORARY PEACOCK BRAND FLOUR LABEL • *See page 21.*

WOMAN CRUSHING SUGAR CANE

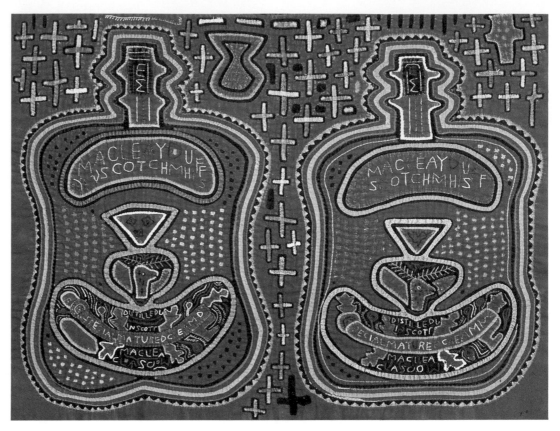

SCOTCH WHISKEY BOTTLES

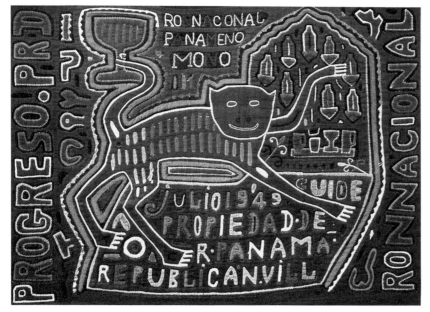

RUM ADVERTISEMENT

VODKA ADVERTISEMENT

224

BLOUSE WITH RUM LABEL • *Liquor labels are often lavish and highly decorative. The artist who made this blouse, the reverse side of which can be seen on page 161, used a Bolivar Rum bottle for inspiration. The appended notation, "Superior quality," which appears on the label, also proclaims a most appropriate judgment of the mola's exquisite workmanship. Together, the two banners have more than 270 cutout circles, each only one-sixteenth of an inch in diameter and tucked under with six tiny stitches. This blouse, a masterpiece of delicate stitchery, dates back to the 1950s; it came from the Carti area, which lies at the upper end of the San Blas Islands chain.*

ANHEUSER-BUSCH BEER MOLA • *Anheuser-Busch's glorified trademark sporting a monumental capital 'A' enmeshed with a spread-winged American eagle clutching a bundle of arrows, is famous among beer drinkers the world over. Equally impressed, but in another way, are the Cuna women who feature it on their molas. This one added her own artistic touch, floral and zoomorphic forms swimming in a sea of laboriously stitched, multicolored cutouts. The lettering reads, "Reg. U.S. Pat. Off., Anheuser-Busch."*

226

ANHEUSER-BUSCH TRADEMARK • *The familiar Anheuser-Busch trademark as it appears on beer-can labels, bottle caps, and shipping cartons.*

LEGENDS FOR FOLLOWING PAGE:

SWEDISH MATCHBOX DESIGN • *The design for this elaborately worked mola was copied from a tiny matchbox cover, as is stated by the somewhat detached lettering on the flowing ribbon in the parrot's talons. Parrot Safety Matches are made in Sweden. The bird is finely stitched, its form kept very close to that of the original, and the broken word "Trademark" is carried proportionately into the design. This artist has used a curious assortment of reptiles and plant forms to fill in open spaces. The minute lettering at the bottom reads, "Made by Jönköpings & Vulcans. T.F.A.B., Sweden."*

PARROT MATCHBOX LABEL • *Photograph of a Parrot Safety Matchbox (actual size) found on the island of Rio Sidra in San Blas. Cunas generally use matches nowadays and seem to prefer the longer-burning wooden variety, most of which are imported to Panama from Sweden. Mola-makers are particularly fond of these brightly colored matchbox labels and frequently use them in blouse designs.*

OLD-FASHIONED FOOD CHOPPER • *This may at first glance appear to be a scattering of the main ingredients for alphabet soup. It is actually a schematic drawing of an old-fashioned food chopper in action. Every detail is carefully noted—the handle, hopper, screw clamp, and grinding mechanism. The jumbled lettering undoubtedly conceals a coherent message, now undecipherable even by the advertising wizard who may have initially conceived it. This mola excells because of its unusual coloring, design, and treatment of subject matter.*

"GOD BLESS AMERICA" MOLA • *Ideas for molas can spring from almost any source. The stereotyped components of this patriotic motif—the Statue of Liberty, eagle with half-furled flag, and emblazoned slogan "God Bless America"—are commonly seen on product labels, souvenir banners, pillows, and other commodities from the Canal Zone.*

227

PARROT MATCHBOX LABEL

SWEDISH MATCHBOX DESIGN

OLD-FASHIONED FOOD CHOPPER

"GOD BLESS AMERICA" MOLA

NEEDLE BOOK COVER

NEEDLE BOOK COVER • *Photograph of an Army and Navy Needle Book with a more modern design, showing an aircraft carrier and jet planes. This is an ordinary brand of sewing needle sold in small shops and street stalls in Panamanian marketplaces.*

DESIGN FROM NEEDLE PACKET • *When the mixed-up lettering on a mola is unscrambled, the way is cleared toward identifying its source. Once the words "Army and Navy Needle Book" are deciphered, it becomes reasonable to assume that this design was copied from a packet of needles, one of the most commonplace items of everyday Cuna life. These inexpensive needle books are made in the Orient and have luridly colored covers, usually of military subjects like this, showing a warship and an airplane flanked by a flag-bearing eagle.*

DESIGN
FROM
NEEDLE
PACKET

229

SINGER SEWING MACHINE MOLA

• *Sewing machines were introduced to San Blas islanders many years ago, but they proved impractical for the intricacies of fine mola-making. Some women do turn out machine-stitched blouses (see page 117), but they are mostly confined to rather simple linear patterns. On the other hand, men use sewing machines for making their traditional shirts (see page 184) and women find them useful for attaching yokes and flounces to their appliquéd panels. The Singer Sewing Machine symbol, now associated with all kinds of sewing, soon became a popular mola motif which is still used occasionally in one or another of its many versions. On this panel the stylized "S" imprinted with the company's totally scrambled name has been reversed to form the other half of an unwieldly serpentine design. Two rigid operators are incorporated into the sinuous double "S" as though caught in the coils of a gigantic snake.*

STORE SIGN IN SAN BLAS VILLAGE

• *Singer products are widely advertised throughout San Blas. An English-language version of this sign, which was posted outside a sparsely stocked village store, may very well have been the prototype for the mola pictured above. It advises that Singer needles and sewing machine oil are sold on the premises.*

230

LEGENDS FOR FOLLOWING PAGE:

The six molas on the following page represent examples from a wide diversity of products which have inspired mola-makers to create new designs. The more fanciful the image, the more it appeals to the Cuna women's sense of color and organization, not to mention their very keen sense of humor. Few Cunas either read or write so the Spanish and English lettering which appears on labels or whatever else they might copy is relatively meaningless.

PETERS COCOA LABEL • *A one-pound Peters Cocoa container, box or tin, was the source for this mola. Particular attention was paid to the central figure, but it is not quite clear whether this Cuna artist saw the serving ladies bringing in trays with cups of steaming hot chocolate or presenting cocoa beans on opened pods.*

KRUPP INDUSTRIAL TRADEMARK • *This famous symbol of Germany's giant steel and armaments industry, the firm of Krupp, probably came to Panama on a packing crate or a piece of machinery. Its visual appeal must have been its resemblance to some of the abstract patterns used on early molas, which were, in turn, derived from ancient body-painting designs.*

McGREGOR CLOTHING LABEL • *This heraldic device showing crowned lions and a knight's visored helmet was copied from a McGregor's Sportswear label. Cuna men wear western-style clothing, so it is not surprising that a windbreaker or jacket with this label should show up in San Blas.*

SHELL OIL COMPANY ADVERTISEMENT • *Because of its bizarre visual impact, this Shell X-100 advertisement influenced not only owners of sluggish cars but Cuna mola-makers as well. As though some modern-day Aladdin had rubbed a magical tow truck, a devilish-looking genie has come forth holding what appears to be a sludge-fouled oil filter which cries out for the company's special lubricant. The producer would no doubt be pleased with this Cuna artist's taking the advertisement one step farther to suggest that the lady at lower left and the one with the umbrella are pedestrians, more than likely set afoot by malfunctioning motors.*

MOBIL OIL CARNIVAL FLOAT • *This Mobil Oil Company advertisement features a carnival float which may have appeared in some pre-Lent or industrial fair parade. The lettering reads "Estrella," or star; "Carro Carnaval," or carnival car; and the product's name is added in English, "Mobil lubrication," "Mobil gas," and "Mobil oil."*

REYNOLDS ALUMINUM TRADEMARK • *This well-known Saint George and the Dragon motif is found all over the globe. Here we see the dauntless warrior astride his noble steed, brandishing a heavy sword, his shield emblazoned with the initial "R," as he vanquishes a very reluctant dragon. This graphically rendered allegorical tale is supposed to symbolize the strength and purity of a mighty product, Reynolds Aluminum. One can be sure that the naïve Indian artist who transformed it into a mola was less interested in the symbolic forces of good and evil than she was in making a beautiful blouse.*

on worldly goods. Cuna women were curious and receptive; product labels were grist for the mola-makers' mill.

Among the earliest advertising designs to appear in large numbers on molas were the RCA Victor Talking Machine trademark (page 240) and a Kools cigarette advertisement (page 234).

Net mending twine had been used by Cuna men for years before one observant and imaginative woman was attracted by the curious fish motif on the spool's label and fashioned it into a mola design which subsequently was copied hundreds of times (page 43).

Safety matches, imported from Europe, were prized by

PETER'S COCOA LABEL

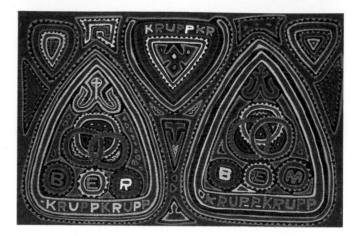

KRUPP INDUSTRIAL TRADEMARK

McGREGOR CLOTHING LABEL

SHELL OIL COMPANY AD

232

MOBIL OIL CARNIVAL FLOAT

REYNOLDS ALUMINUM TRADEMARK

EFFICIENCY CIGARETTES MOLA

EFFICIENCY CIGARETTES MOLA • *It is difficult to see what this Crucifixion scene with its Black Christ and foliated cross has to do with Efficiency Cigarettes, but one Cuna Indian woman liked the design enough to stitch it onto her blouse.*

VICEROY CIGARETTE PACKAGES • *These out-of-perspective Viceroy cigarette packages with their protruding filter tips are repeated in miniature on the side of each pack, perhaps for the benefit of the encapsulated figures lingering alongside.*

MULTIPLE CIGARETTE AD • *Two giant roosters with brilliant plumage, paired off as though in a fighting stance, dominate this "propaganda mola," which expressly advertises three brands of cigarettes—Philip Morris, Marlboro, and Gallito. The bottom line of lettering states that they are Hechos en Panama (Made in Panama). The boldly lettered slogan "Finos hasta el final" means essentially "Good to the last puff."*

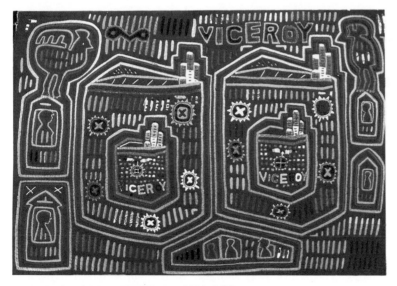

VICEROY CIGARETTE PACKAGES

MULTIPLE CIGARETTE AD

233

KOOL CIGARETTES • *A fondly remembered advertising campaign from a generation ago featured Willie the Penguin promoting Kool cigarettes and was one of the earliest cigarette ads to be reflected in the mola world. It is doubtful that Cuna artists ever understood the idea connecting penguins with a cool smoke. On this complicated design the all-too-familiar Willie of "Smoke Kools" fame is seen lighting up. A large packet of Kool cigarettes separates him from a long-beaked companion. At the top of the design is the commanding phrase, "Willie the Penguin says smoke Penguins" or Penquinos, as Kools were called in the Latin-American marketplace. Many molas were made using variations of this amusing but insidious theme. Occasionally, a faded and torn example can still be found, cast off into the corner of some darkened hut—all that remains of a forgotten fad from a bygone era.*

234

the women not only for their quick light but for their brightly colored box labels as well. One brand, Parrot Matches, had special appeal because it pictured an already familiar and favorite mola subject which could be, and soon was, gloriously transposed into a beautiful blouse design (page 228).

On the islands where bread was first baked in the 1930s, milled white flour was brought in by the sackful. Printed on some of these cotton bags were eye-catching pictorial brand labels, at least one of which was transformed into a radiant mola (page 221). When airstrips were built, tourists came with a thirst for soft drinks and beer, already discovered by Cunas and stocked in island trading posts. Mola-makers got twice as much for their nickels when they stitched the bottle labels to their blouses (page 226).

Pedal sewing machines were brought to San Blas many years ago and men used them to make clothing for themselves and their sons, and as more machines became available, the women learned to rely on them for stitching together the component parts of blouses. They also turned to the Singer trademark as a design source and for a time blouses were produced with endless variations of that company's stylized *S*.

At first the influx of exciting new images was sufficient to generate a resurgence of mola art. The women had plenty of material to choose from, with all the different objects then being introduced into island life. As the practice of using nonindigenous imagery grew, the Cuna imagination expanded and artists became eager to collect and use designs from products that would not normally reach San Blas. They attempted interpretations of advertisements they found in magazines and other printed matter. These heady experiments resulted in images like

LEGENDS FOR FOLLOWING PAGE:

LIONS CLUB DESIGN • *In the early 1970s the International Lions Club held its annual meeting of the board in Panama City. The event received wide coverage by the media, and the club's emblem showed up all over the city. The Cuna's love of depicting wild animals on their molas made this a natural for interpretation. Note how the original design is enriched by the addition of various types of fauna, especially the lively creature which replaces the giant initial "L" in the center, which the Cuna artist must have found a meaningless and clumsy shape.*

LIONS CLUB EMBLEM • *One does not have to be a member of the club to recognize this internationally famous emblem. Its double lion-headed image was as appealing to the Cuna Indian woman who copied it for the mola opposite as it could be for any loyal member of the Lions Club.*

KELLOGG'S CEREAL BOX • *This Frosted Flakes box shows the same "Tony, the Tiger" motif which inspired the mola next to it. By comparing the similarities and differences between the two, much can be learned about the Cuna's creative process of transposing a design from another medium into mola stitchery.*

TONY, THE TIGER • *Kellogg's "Tony, the Tiger" was the design source for this amusing mola. The familiar face of that company's mascot has been pictured on several different breakfast cereal boxes in recent years. Although not the usual fare on a Cuna breakfast menu, corn flakes, which were formerly brought from Panama or the Canal Zone, are now available at trading posts on some of the larger San Blas islands. A Cuna woman might buy a box not only for its contents but for the tiger design too.*

LIONS CLUB EMBLEM

LIONS CLUB DESIGN

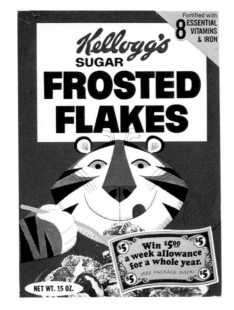

KELLOGG'S CEREAL BOX

TONY THE TIGER

236

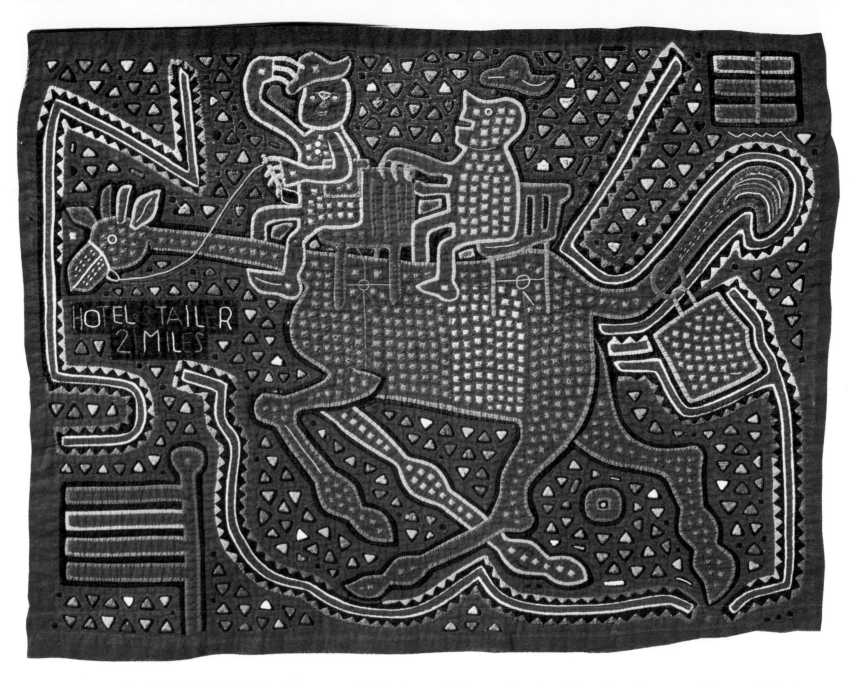

HOTEL STATLER ADVERTISEMENT • *Shown on this finely worked mola is a galloping giraffe with two safari types being jauntily bounced along in chairs tied to his back, their luggage gaily looped over his tail. The sign reads "HOTEL STATLER, 21 MILES," correct except for an incomplete T. This droll tableau harks back to a clever advertising campaign waged by the hotel chuin, which graphically suggested in a variety of captivating ways* *that no matter how far a traveler strayed from civilization there was always the luxurious comfort of a Statler within reasonable reach. The reverse side (not shown) carries a design showing a wartime anti-Japanese propaganda cartoon topped by the COLLIER'S logo, which provided the clue to date its source as a magazine advertisement from the World War II era.*

237

BIRD WITH TELEVISION SET • *When the source for a mola design can be located, even one as insignificant as this cartoonlike bird holding a television set, the Cuna artist's thought process can be studied. Tiny details that pleased the mola-maker, such as the heart on the toucan's beak, are retained whereas unnecessary or unattractive details such as the lettering, in this case, are eliminated. The formless feet and the TV set's uninteresting control panel pictured in the original ad are elaborated upon for the blouse.*

ADVERTISEMENT FOR TV SET • *Originally a full-color advertisement for HITACHI integrated circuit color television sets, this picture was printed, among other places, in a bilingual vacation and shopping guide called "Focus on Panama," published twice a year by the Panamanian Tourist Office and available free to tourists and other interested parties. The 1972 issue in which this advertisement appeared carried a special feature article on a Cuna hotel in Ailigandi where this mola was made. Since numerous copies of the guide turned up in that area of San Blas, it is not presumptuous to assume that this was the mola's immediate design source.*

TV CHANNEL 2 LOGO • *Fish are one of the more common mola motifs. They are made in large numbers and come in infinite variety. Most are just marine-life shapes, but many are perfectly identifiable and some are even labeled so there can be no mistaking them. Once encountered it seems only natural that a Cuna woman would choose the fish-form lettering of Panama's Channel 2 TV logo to decorate her blouse.*

the "Shell Oil Ad" (page 232), the "Rum Advertisement" and "Vodka Advertisement" (page 224), and the "Soft Drink" and "Vermouth Advertisement" (page 220).

When a Cuna artist copies an advertisement or product label onto a mola panel, she does it because something in the design catches her fancy. She has little understanding that it is propaganda which is supposed to lure her into buying the product. Her delight is with the novel idea, for instance, of a man drinking through five straws at once (page 220). In the "Aluminum Ad" at the bottom of page 232, the artist carefully renders the Saint George and the Dragon theme onto a blouse and decides what size and color to make the letters in "Reynolds Aluminum," but she is unaware of what the letters mean, what aluminum is, or why she should be impressed with its strength. And so it is with hundreds of designs of this type. Many Cuna women still think advertising art is purely for decoration.

For those of us who take for granted that the medium is the message, it might require a shifting of gears before we can fully comprehend that mola-makers have not the slightest idea of the intentions behind all those advertising labels and slogans . . . and care even less!

BIRD WITH
TELEVISION
SET

AD FOR TV SET

TV CHANNEL 2
LOGO

239

PHONOGRAPH RECORD LABEL

RCA VICTOR ADVERTISEMENT

240   BELL SYSTEM MOLA

TELEVISION MOLA

PHONOGRAPH RECORD LABEL • *Two world-renowned musical figures are presented on this Victor Red Seal collector's item—Italian tenor Enrico Caruso, and the even more famous Nipper, RCA's canine mascot, whose head-cocked image on the company's trademark became so familiar.*

RCA VICTOR ADVERTISEMENT • *For popularity the "His Master's Voice" motif has enjoyed one of the longest runs of any mola design. Most widely used during the 1950s, it is still occasionally made. Some versions are extremely crude, almost to the point of abstraction, while others tend toward stylization. However, most remain representational, and many of the better examples have a highly sophisticated look. This red-eyed Nipper, although still pretending attentiveness, has grown out of proportion and acquired a few spots, suggesting that he has concentrated more on eating his Kennel Rations than harking to his master's voice. The minions in attendance are busily employed keeping the phonograph functioning properly for the big dog's pleasure. The "RCA Victor, Reg." trademark is prominently displayed and the belled horn is inscribed with the words "Panama Radio."*

BELL SYSTEM MOLA • *Sometimes the figures stitched onto a mola make very little sense except in their remarkable organization and unusual color combinations. This panel exhibits a hodgepodge of common design elements which have been neatly arranged to fit into a minimum of space. At the left is what seems to be a vintage-model radio with its morning glory speaker mounted on top, slightly reminiscent of the early phonographs pictured on RCA Victor advertisements. The bird perched atop a bell captioned "Bell System" probably denotes that company's Panamanian telephone service. More amusing is the touching vignette at lower right where one beady-eyed, Audubon-oriented person holds up another as though offering him as a tasty morsel to the alert seabird stopped in mid-flight.*

TELEVISION MOLA • *United States television programs are broadcast regularly from the Canal Zone, and Cunas can often be seen among the knots of curious people watching flickering sets operating in shop windows. This design was not made strictly for tourists but was worn by the woman who stitched it. It features a console model TV set, garnished with knobs and feet, showing the familiar RCA Victor motif in full color on the screen. This time an aging Nipper, perhaps a little hard of hearing by now, is listening through the bulbous horn of an old-time phonograph, aided by a plugged-in earphone device.*

HIS MASTER'S VOICE • *RCA Victor's patient little fox terrier Nipper has been listening to his master's voice since 1901. Painted by a London artist, Francis Barraud, the original canvas was sold to William Barry Owen, head of England's Gramaphone Company. He, in turn, sold the American rights to the Victor Talking Machine Company where it was used extensively as the company's trademark in advertising and on their Red Seal Records series. The "talking dog", as it was erroneously but affectionately called, soon became one of the world's most familiar product symbols and a natural for mola-makers who were entranced by the musical sounds produced by early wind-up phonographs.*

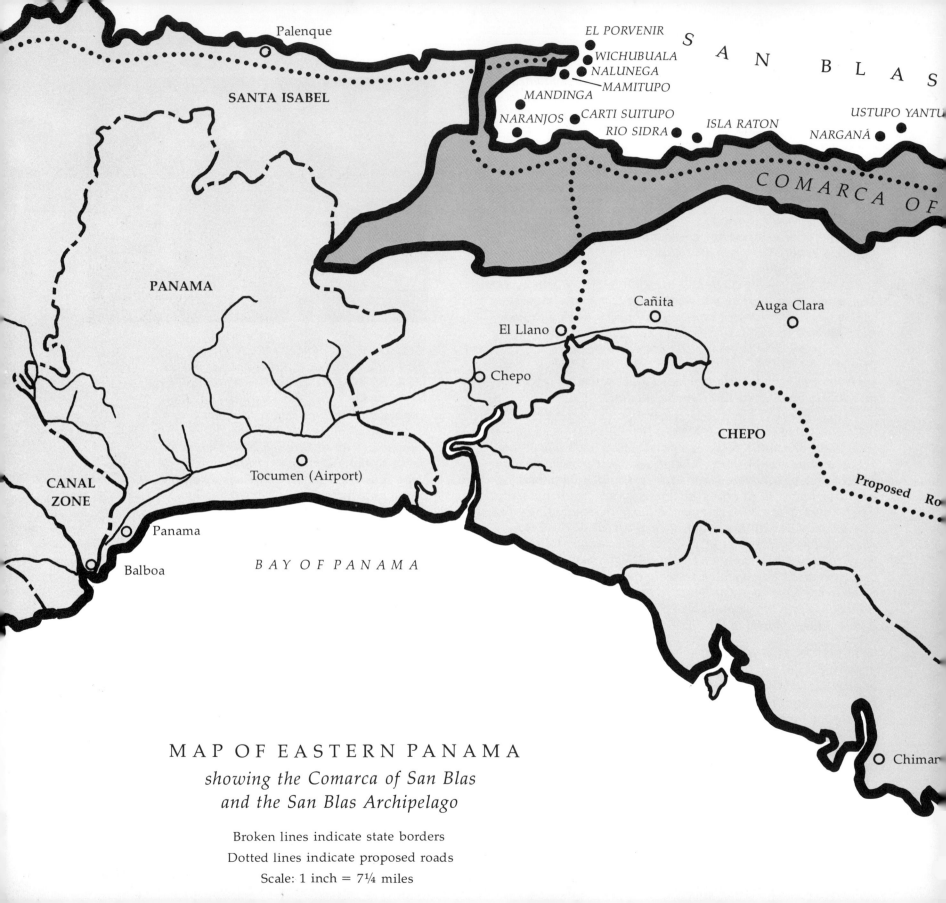

MAP OF EASTERN PANAMA
*showing the Comarca of San Blas
and the San Blas Archipelago*

Broken lines indicate state borders
Dotted lines indicate proposed roads
Scale: 1 inch = 7¼ miles

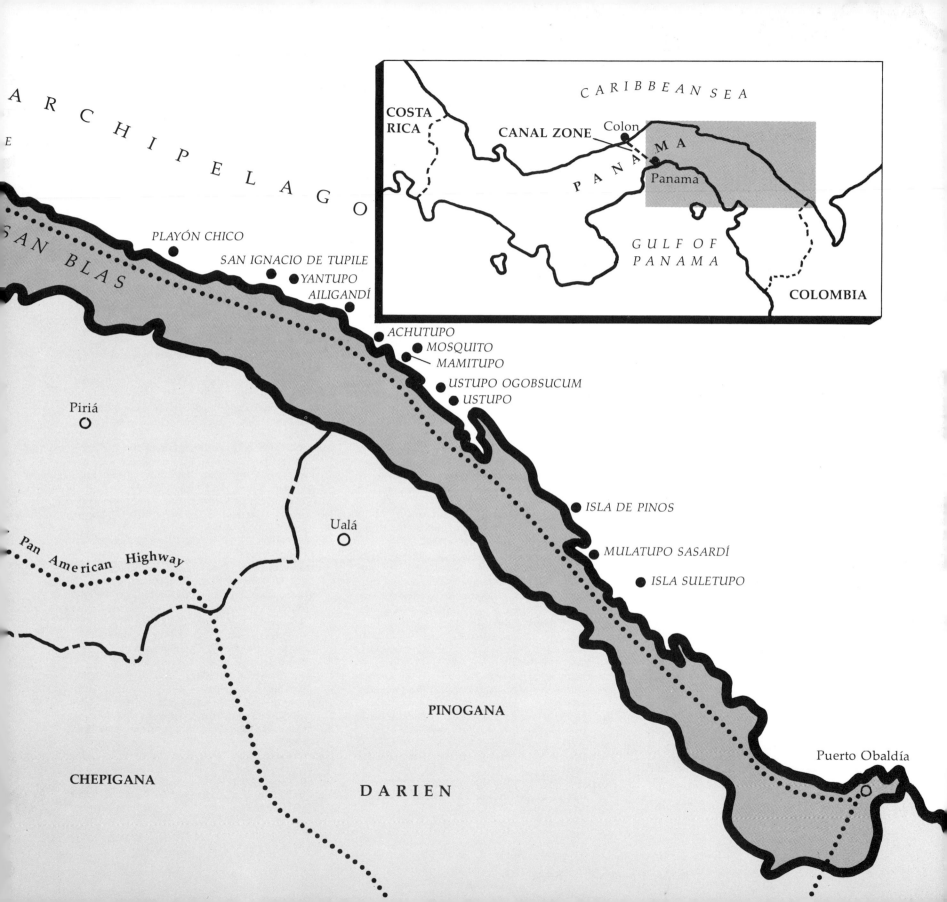

ARCHIPELAGO

SAN BLAS

PLAYÓN CHICO

SAN IGNACIO DE TUPILE

YANTUPO
AILIGANDÍ

ACHUTUPO

MOSQUITO
MAMITUPO

USTUPO OGOBSUCUM
USTUPO

Piriá

Ualá

Pan American Highway

ISLA DE PINOS

MULATUPO SASARDÍ

ISLA SULETUPO

PINOGANA

CHEPIGANA

D A R I E N

Puerto Obaldía

CARIBBEAN SEA

COSTA RICA

CANAL ZONE   Colon

P A N A M A

Panama

GULF OF PANAMA

COLOMBIA

Bibliography

A random gathering of bibliographical references to the Cuna Indians, their land, their historical background, and their molas.

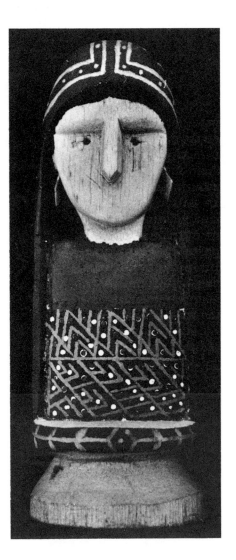

244 POLYCHROMED FIGURE, FRONT

ABBOT, WILLIS, JR. *Panama and the Canal in Picture and Prose.* New York: 1913.

"About Molas." *Panama Canal Press,* 1969.

ACOSTA, JOAQUIN. *Compendio Histórico del Descubrimiento y Colonización de la Nueva Granada en el Siglo Decimo Sexto.* Paris: 1848.

AGUADO, FRAY PEDRO. *Recopilación Histórica Escrito en el Siglo 16, y Publicada Ahora por Primer Vez.* Bogota: 1906

ALBA, MANUEL MARÍA. "Entología y Población Histórica de Panama." *Geografía Descriptivo de la Republica de Panama.* Panama: 1928.

———. *Hombres y Dióses Cunas: La Creación del Mundo Cuna.* Panama: 1947.

ANDAGOYA, PASCUAL DE. Narrative of the Proceedings of Pedrarias Dávila in the Provinces of Tierra Firme or Castilla del Oro, and of the Discovery of the South Sea and the Coasts of Peru and Nicaragua. London: 1865.

———. "Relación de los Sucesos de Pedrarias Dávila en las Provincias de Tierra Firme o Castilla del Oro." *Jijon y Caamano.* 1936–1938.

ANDERSON, CHARLES L. G. *Life and Letters of Vasco Nuñez de Balboa.* New York: 1941.

———. *Old Panama and Castilla del Oro.* Boston: 1914.

ARÉVALO, ANTONIO. "Descripción o Relación del Golfo del Darien, 1761." *Col. Doc. Ined. Geogr. Hist.* Colombia, 1891–1894.

AULD, RHODA L. *Molas, What They Are, How to Make Them, Ideas They Suggest for Creative Appliqué.* New York: 1977.

BANCROFT, HUBERT HOWE. *History of Central America* (vols. 6 to 8 of the *Works*), vol. 1. San Francisco, 1883–1890.

———. *The Native Races of the Pacific States of North America.* Vol. 1, *Wild Tribes.* New York, 1875.

———. *The Native Races of the Pacific States of North America.* Vol. 5, *Primitive History.* San Francisco, 1883.

BARRETT, JOHN. "Facts About Panama." *Monthly Bulletin of the Bureau of American Republics,* February 1904.

———. "Facts about Panama." *U.S. Consular Reports,* 1904.

———. Historical Sketch of the Isthmus of Panama (in Spanish). *Monthly Bulletin of the Bureau of American Republics,* July 1904.

BELL, ELEANOR YORKE. "The Republic of Panama and Its People with Special Reference to the Indians." *Annual Report of the Smithsonian Institution.* Washington: 1909.

BIESANZ, JOHN and MAVIS. *The People of Panama.* New York: 1955.

BOLLAERT, WILLIAM. "Ancient Indian Tombs of Chiriqui, etc." *American Ethnological Society Transactions,* vol. 2.

BORLAND, REV. FRANCIS. *The History of Darien, Giving a Short Description of That Country and an Account of the Attempts of the Scotch Nation to Settle a Colony There, etc.* Glasgow: 1779.

BRINTON, D. G. *The American Race.* New York: 1891.

BROWN, LADY RICHMOND. *Unknown Tribes, Uncharted Seas.* London: 1924.

BURNEY, JAMES. *History of the Buccaneers of America.* London: 1891.

BURR, WILLIAM H. "The Republic of Panama." *National Geographic Magazine,* February 1904

CANADAY, JOHN. "Artistry Via Needle from Panama Islands—Artistry Sewn by Cuna Women." *New York Times,* 30 December 1968

———. "Mea Culpa." *New York Times,* 8 August 1971.

CARLES, RUBEN DARIO. "El Archipiélago de San Blas, Tierra de Los Cunas." Panama: 1965.

———. "San Blas Millenary Land of the Cunas." Panama: n. d. (1965?).

CATLIN, STANTON L., and HOOVER, F. LOUIS. "Molas from the San Blas Islands." Exhibition catalogue, Center for Inter-American Relations. New York: 1968.

CHAPIN, MAC. "Pab Igala: Historias de la Tradición Kuna." *Centro de Investigaciónes Antropológicas.* Panama: 1970.

CHAVES, ENRIQUE, and ANGERMULLER, LINNEA. *About Molas.* Panama: 1972.

CHEN, ALBERTO CHAN, and BENJAMIN, MALCOLM. "Panama Handicrafts." *Senapi.* Panama: 1970.

CHEVILLE, LILA R., and RICHARD A. *Festivals and Dances of Panama.* Panama: 1977.

COLUMBUS, CHRISTOPHER (COLOMBO, CRISTOFORO). *The Voyages of Christopher Columbus, Being the Journals of His First and Third and the Letters Concerning His First and Last Voyages, to Which Is Added the Account of His Second Voyage Written by Andrés Bernáldez: Now Newly Translated and Edited with an Introduction and Notes by Cecil Jane.* London: 1930.

———. *Select Documents Illustrating the Four Voyages of Columbus, Including Those Contained in R. H. Major's Select Letters of Christopher Columbus, Translated and Edited with Additional Material, etc.* London: 1930–1933.

COOKE, HEREWARD LESTER. *Molas: Art of the Cuna Indians.* Exhibition Catalogue for the Textile Museum. Washington: 1973.

COOPE, ANNA. *Anna Coope, Sky Pilot of the San Blas Islands.* New York: 1931.

CORIN, GEORGIA. "All About Molas." *Panama Canal Review* (Special Edition). Panama: n. d. (1970s).

Costa Rica-Panama Arbitration Documents Annexed to the Argument of Costa Rica Before the Arbitrator Hon. Edward Douglass White, Chief Justice of the United States. 4 vols. Rosslyn, Va.: 1913.

CREIGHTON, J. M. "A Hermit Tribe—The San Blas Indians of Panama." *The Mentor,* February 1925.

CRIADO DE CASTILLA, ALONSO. *Summary Description of the Kingdom of Tierra Firme, Called Castilla del Oro, Which Is Subject to the Royal Audiencia of the City of Panama, etc., 1575.* Panama: 1913.

CULLEN, DR. EDWARD. *Isthmus of Darien Ship Canal.* London: 1853.

DAMPIER, WILLIAM. *A New Voyage Around the World.* London: 1699.

DENIKER, J. *The Races of Men.* London: 1901.

DENSMORE, FRANCIS. *Music of the Tule Indians of Panama.* Washington: 1926.

DE SMIDT, LEON S. *Among the San Blas Indians of Panama.* Troy, N.Y.: 1948.

DOCKSTADER, FREDERICK J. *Indian Art in Middle America.* Greenwich, Conn.; 1964.

ESQUEMELING, JOHN. *The Buccaneers of America.* London: 1911.

FEENEY, CORINNE B. "Arch-Isolationists, the San Blas Indians." *National Geographic Magazine,* February 1941.

FERNÁNDEZ DURO, CESÁREO, et. al., eds. *Colección de Documentos Inéditos Relativos al Descubrimiento, Conquista y Organización de las Antiguas Posesiones Españolas de Ultramar.* 25 vols. Madrid: 1885–1932.

FLORES, PEDRO. *Inquiry Concerning the Merits and Services of Captain Pedro Flores Cartago, 1611.* Costa Rica: 1881 and 1907.

GABB, W. M. Paper on Indian Tribes and Languages of Costa Rica, etc. Read before the Philosophical Society, Philadelphia, 20 August 1875.

GAGE, THOMAS. *A New Survey of the West Indies, 1648.* New York: 1929.

GARAY, NARCISO. *Tradiciones y Cantares de Panama.* Belgium: 1930.

GASSÓ, LEONARDO. *La Misión de San José de Narganá Entra los Karibes* (vols. 18–22). Barcelona: 1910 and 1914.

GAUSE, FRANK A., and CARR, CHARLES CARL. *The Story of Panama, the New Route to India.* Boston: 1912.

GEETING, CORINNE. "A Culture Sewn up by Its Women." *Weekender Magazine* (Sacramento Union), 10 February 1973.

———. "The Mystique of the Mola, Sculptures in Cloth." *Westart,* 3 November 1972.

GILLSÁTER, SVEN. *From Island to Island.* London: 1968.

GISBORNE, LIONEL. *The Isthmus of Darien in 1852.* London: 1853.

GONZALEZ GUZMAN, RAUL. "Ritos de Passaje Femenino Entra Los Indios Cunas." *Actos del III Simpósium Nacional de Antropología, Arqueología, y Etnohistoria de Panama.* Panama: December 1972.

HALE, H. C. *Notes on Panama.* Washington: 1903.

HARRINGTON, RICHARD. "San Blas Indians of Panama." *Canadian Geographic Journal* 37, no. 1, (1957).

HARRIS, REGINALD G. "The San Blas Indians." *American Journal of Physical Anthropology* 9, no. 1 (1926).

HOLMER, NILS M. *Critical and Comparative Grammar of the Cuna Language.* Göteborg: 1947.

———. "Cuna Chrestomathy." *Etnologiska Studier* no. 18. Göteborg; 1951.

———. "Ethno-Linguistic Cuna Dictionary." *Etnologiska Studier* no. 19. Göteborg: 1952.

——— and WASSÉN, HENRY. *Mu-Igala or the Way of Muu, a Medicine Song from the Cuna Indians.* Göteborg: 1947.

HOLMES, WILLIAM HENRY. "Ancient Art of the Province of Chiriqui." 6th Annual Report, Bureau of Ethnology. Washington: 1888.

———. *The Use of Gold and Other Metals Among the Ancient Inhabitants of Chiriqui, Isthmus of Darien.* Washington: 1887.

HOLZ, LORETTA, and POESE, BILL. "Make a Mukan Mola." *Popular Crafts* 2, no. 8 (1973).

HOOVER, LOUIS. "Molas from the San Blas Islands." New York: 1968.

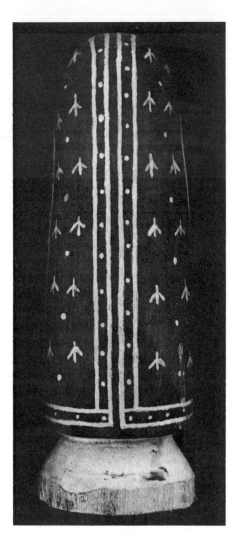

POLYCHROMED FIGURE, BACK

HOST, PER. *Children of the Jungle.* London: 1956.

HUMPHRIES, FRANK T. *The Indians of Panama, Their History, and Culture.* Panama: 1944.

INSH, GEORGE PRATT. *The Company of Scotland Trading to Africa and the Indies.* New York: 1932.

JOHNSON, F. "Central American Cultures: An Introduction." *Handbook of South American Indians,* vol. 5. Washington: 1948.

JOYCE, L. E. *Wafer's Description of the Isthmus of Panama.* London: 1934.

JUAN, DON JORGE, and ULLOA, DON ANTONIO. *Relacion Histórica del Viaje a La America Meridional.* Madrid: 1748.

KAPP, KIT S. *The Early Maps of Panama to 1825.* London: 1971.

———. *Mola Art from the San Blas Islands.* North Bend, Ohio: 1972.

KEELER, CLYDE E. *Apples of Immortality from the China Tree of Life.* New York: 1961.

———. *Cuna Indian Art: the Culture and Craft of Panama's San Blas Islanders.* New York: 1969.

———. "Cuna Indian Beliefs Concerning the Afterlife." *Journal, Tenn. Academy of Science* 29 (1954).

———. "Cuna Uchus and Catholic Saints." *Journal, Tenn. Academy of Science* 30 (1955).

———. *Land of the Moon-Children, the Primitive San Blas Culture in Flux.* Athens: 1956.

———. "More About Uchus in San Blas." *Journal, Tenn. Academy of Science* 31 (1956).

———. *Secrets of the Cuna Earthmother.* New York: 1960.

———. "The Burial of a Cuna Indian Girl." *Journal, Tenn. Academy of Science* 29 (1954).

———. "The Worship of Ishtar Among the Cuna Indians of San Blas." *Bulletin, Georgia Academy of Science* 14 (1956).

———. "Want to Buy a San Blas Mola Blouse?" *Month in Panama,* February 1965.

KELLY, JOANNE M. *Cuna.* New York: 1966.

KINNEY, BOB, ed. "Extensive Inaugural Exhibit Focuses on Art and Artifacts of Cuna Indians." Granville, Ohio: November 1976.

KRIEGER, HERBERT W. *Material Culture of the People of Southeastern Panama, Based on Specimens in the U.S. National Museum.* Washington: 1926.

"Kuna Indian Art." Illustrated flyer, 1976.

LAUREY, J. R. "Cut-through work." *Appliqué Stitchery.* New York: 1966.

LEONARD, JONATHAN. *Molas from the San Blas Islands.* (Exhibition catalogue.) Washington: n. d. (early 1970s).

LINDSAY, FORBES. *Panama—the Isthmus and the Canal.* Philadelphia: 1906.

LINNÉ, SIGVALD. *Darien in the Past: the Archaeology of Eastern Panama and Northwestern Colomzia.* Göteborg: 1929.

LOTHROP, SAMUEL KIRKLAND. *Coclé, an Archaeological Study of Central Panama* (Part 1). Cambridge: 1937.

———. *Coclé, an Archaeological Study of Central Panama* (Part 2). Cambridge: 1942.

———. *The Discovery of Gold in the Graves of Chiriqui.* Panama: 1919.

LUTZ, O. *Die Ureinwohner am Isthmus von Panama.* Stuttgart: 1922.

MCANDREWS, ANITA. "Ibe-or-Cuna (unpublished manuscript), 1970s.

MACCURDY, GEORGE GRANT. *A Study of Chiriquian Antiquities.* New Haven: 1911.

MCKIM, FRED. *San Blas, an Account of the Cuna Indians of Panama* and *The Forbidden Land; Reconnaissance of the Upper Bayano River, Republic of Panama.* Göteborg: 1947.

MANN, JOHN. *Text of a Talk on the Cuna Indians of San Blas* (typescript). Panama: 1974.

MARSH, RICHARD O. *White Indians of Darien.* New York: 1934.

MATTIL, EDWARD L. "The Cuna Mola." *Everyday Art* (Spring). Sandusky, Ohio: 1974.

MEINHOLD, ALBERTO C. *La Republic de Panama.* Santiago: 1906.

MORGAN, CHRISTINE HUDGINS. *I Married a San Blas Indian.* New York: 1958.

MORNER, KATHLEEN. "Progress vs. Panama's Cuna Indians." *Midwest Magazine,* 20 April 1969.

NEAL, AVON, and PARKER, ANN. "Madison Avenue's Secret Conquest." *American Heritage,* June 1974.

——— and PARKER, ANN. "Molas: Jungle View of 'Civilization.' " *Smithsonian,* November 1975.

——— and PARKER, ANN. "The Witchery of Stitchery." *Ciba Journal* (Spring). Basle, Switzerland: 1968.

NELSON, WOLFRED. *Five Years at Panama.* New York: 1899.

NEWTON, DOLORES, and RIPP, WENDY. *Mola: Reverse Appliqué from the San Blas Islands.* Long Island, N.Y.: 1973.

NICHOLAS, FRANCIS C. *Around the Caribbean and Across Panama.* Boston: 1903.

———. "Panama and Its People." *Review of Reviews,* March 1904.

NORDENSKIÖLD, ERLAND. "An Historical and Ethnological Survey of the Cuna Indians." *Com. Ethnogr. Stud.* 10. Göteborg: 1938.

———. "Cuna Indian Religion." *Proc. of the 23rd Intern. Congr. of Americanists.* New York: 1930.

———. *Indianerna på Panamanäset.* Stockholm: 1928.

———. "Les Indiens de l'Isthme de Panama." *La Geogr.* Paris: 1928.

———. "Les Rapports entre l'Art, la Religion et la Magie chez les Indiens Cuna et Choco." *Journ. Soc. Amer.* 21. Paris: 1929.

———. "Picture-writings and Other Documents, etc." *Comp. Ethnogr. Stud.* 7. Göteborg: 1928–1930.

OTIS, F. N. *Isthmus of Panama, etc.* New York: 1867.

OVIEDO Y VALDÉS, GONZALO FERNÁNDEZ DE. *Historia General y Natural de las Indias, Islas y Tierra Firme de la Mar Oceano* (4 vols.). Madrid: 1851–55.

"Paradise Awakening: The San Blas Islands." *Panama Canal Review*, 15 February 1965.

PARKER, ANN. *Outside Influences on the Design of San Blas Indian Molas.* Paper given at Textile Museum's "Mesa Redonda," April 1976, Washington.

PASADA, FRANCISCO. *Colombia.* London: 1822.

———. *Directorio General de la Ciudad de Panama y Reseña Histórica Geografía 7 del Departmente.* Panama: 1898.

PENSA, HENRI. *La Republique et le Canal.* Paris: 1906.

PERALTA, MANUEL MARIA DE. *Costa Rica, Nicaragua y Panama en el Siglo XVI, etc.* Madrid: 1883.

PIM, BEDFORD, and SEEMAN, BARTHOLD. *Dottings on the Roadside in Panama, Nicaragua, and Mosquito.* London: 1867.

PINART, ALPHONSE LOUIS. "Chiriqui: Bocas del Toro—Valle Miranda." *Bull. Soc. Geogr.* 6. Paris: 1885.

———. *Colección de Linguística y Etnografía Americanas,* vol. 4. San Francisco: 1882.

———. "Les Indiens de l'Etat de Panama." *Revue d'Ethnographie* (March–April) Paris: 1887.

———. *Notes sur les Limites de Civilization de l'Isthme Americain.* Washington: n. d.

———. *Notes sur les Tribus Indiennes de Familles Guarano-Guaymies de l'Isthme de Panama et du Centre-Amerique.* Chartres: 1900.

———. *Vocabulario Castellano-Cuna, etc.* Paris: 1890.

PINCHOT, GIFFORD. *To the South Seas.* Philadelphia: 1930.

PITTIER, H. H. "Little Known Parts of Panama." *National Geographic Magazine* 23, no. 7 (1912).

PREBBLE, JOHN. *The Darien Disaster, a Scots Colony in the New World, 1698–1700.* New York: 1968.

PRESTÁN, ARNULFO. *El Use de la Chicha y la Sociedad Kuna.* Mexico: 1975.

PRICE, JAMES L. *Jungle Jim.* New York: 1941.

PRINCE, J. DYNELEY. "A Text in the Indian Language of Panama-Darien." *American Anthropologist* 15 (1913).

PUIG, MANUEL MARIA. *Diccionario de la Lengua Cuna.* Panama: 1944.

———. *Los Indios Cunas de San Blas.* Panama: 1947.

RECLUS, ARMAND. *Panama et Darien Voyages d'Exploration, 1876–1878.* Paris: 1888.

REQUEJO SALCEDO, JUAN. "Relación Histórica y Geográfica de la Provincia de Panama—1640." *Col. Libr. Doc. Ref. Hist. Amer.* Madrid: 1908.

RESTREPO TIRADO, ERNESTO. *Estudios Sobre los Aborígenes de Colombia.* Bogota: 1892.

———. "Un Viaje al Darien." *loteria*, July, 1961.

"Reverse Appliqué." *Woman's Day*, May 1966.

REVERTE, JOSE MANUEL. *El Matrimónio Entre los Indios Cuna de Panama.* Panama: 1966.

———. *Rio Bayano.* Panama: 1961.

ROSEN, STEVEN W. "Art and Artifacts of the San Blas Cuna." (Exhibition catalogue.) Grandville, Ohio: 1976.

———. "The Two Year Tale of the Transfer of General MacArthur and Thirteen Other Uchus to Denison" and "The Cuna Collection." *Denison Alumnus* (Winter). Granville, Ohio: 1974.

RUIZ DE CAMPOS, DIEGO. *Relación Sobre la Costa Panameña en al Mar de Sur por el Capitán Diego Ruíz de Campos Año de 1631.*

SAUER, CARL ORTWIN. *The Early Spanish Main.* Berkeley: 1966.

SEEMAN, BERTHOLD. "The Aborigines of the Isthmus of Panama." *Transactions of the Amer. Ethn. Soc.* 3. New York: 1853.

SELFRIDGE, COMMANDER T. O. *Report of Explorations and Surveys for a ship Canal, Isthmus of Panama.* Washington: 1874.

———. *Stanford's Compendium of Geography* (Central and South America), vols. 1 and 2. London: 1901.

SEVERIN, KURT. "San Blas Puberty Party." *Safari* (April). Jersey City: 1956.

SEVERIN, TIMOTHY. *The Horizon Book of Vanishing Primitive Man.* New York: 1973.

SMITH, BRADLEY. *Columbus in the New World.* Garden City, N.Y.: 1962.

STONE, DORIS. "Synthesis of Lower Central American Ethnohistory." *Handbook of Middle American Indians.* Austin: 1966.

STOUT, DAVID B. "Persistent Elements in San Blas Cuna Social Organization." 29th International Congress of Americanists, 1952.

———. *San Blas Acculturation: an Introduction.* New York: 1947.

———. "The Cuna." *Handbook of South American Indians,* vol. 4. Washington: 1948.

"The Appliqués of San Blas." *Craft Horizons*, January and February 1960.

TINNIN, J. V. *Roughing It in the San Blas Islands.* Panama: 1940.

TOMES, ROBERT. *Panama in 1855.* New York: 1855.

TORRES DE ARAUZ, REINA C. "Aspectos Culturales de los Indios Cunas." *Anuario de Estudios Americanos* 15. (1958).

———. *Darien Etnoecología de Una Región Histórica.* Panama: 1975.

———. "Etnohistória Cuna." *Loteria*, July 1974.

———. *La Mujer Cuna de Panama.* Mexico: 1957.

PRACTICE BEADWORK DESIGN

VALDES, RAMON M. *Geografía del Istmo de Panama.* Bogota: 1890.

———. *Geografía del Istmo de Panama, etc.* New York: 1905.

VANDERVELDE, M. M. *Keep Out of Paradise.* Nashville: 1966.

VERRILL, ALPHEUS HYATT. *Excavations in Coclé Province.* Panama: 1927.

———. *Panama, Past & Present.* New York: 1921.

VILLEGAS, SABAS A. *The Republic of Panama.* Panama: 1917.

WAFER, LIONEL. *A New Voyage and Description of the Isthmus of America, 1699.* Cleveland, Ohio: 1903.

WASSÉN, HENRY. "An Analogy Between a South American and Oceanic Myth Motif and Negro Influence in Darien." *Etnologiska Studier,* no. 10. Göteborg: 1940.

———. "Anonymous Spanish Manuscript from 1739 on the Province of Darien." *Etnologiska Studier,* no. 10. Göteborg: 1940.

———. "Contributions to Cuna Ethnography; Results of an Expedition to Panama and Colombia in 1947." *Etnologiska Studier,* no. 16. Göteborg: 1949.

———. "Cuentos de los Indios Chocos, etc." *Journ. Soc. Amer.* 25. Paris: 1933.

———. "Mitos y Cuentos de los Indios Cunas" *Journ. Soc. Amer.* 26. Paris: 1934.

———. *Mola, Cuna-Indiansk Textilkonst.* Göteborg: 1968.

———. "Original Documents from the Cuna Indians of San Blas, etc." *Etnologiska Studier,* no. 6. Göteborg: 1938.

———. "Some Cuna Indian Animal Stories with Original Texts" *Etnologiska Studier,* no. 4. Göteborg: 1937.

———. "Some Words on the Cuna Indians and Especially their 'Mola' Garments." *Revista do Museo Paulista* (Nova serie, vol. 15). São Paulo, Brazil: 1964.

———. "The Complete Mu-Igala in Picture Writing." *Etnologiska Studier.* vol. 21.

WEIL, THOMAS E., et al. *Area Handbook for Panama.* Washington: 1972.

WEYER, EDWARD, JR. *Primitive Peoples Today.* Garden City, N.Y.: n. d. (1958).

WILLIAMS, VINNIE. "He Collects Indian Blouses." *The Atlanta Journal & Constitution,* 16 May 1968.

WYSE, L. N. B. *Carte General.* 1885.

———. War Department Map, April 1909.

Sources

Molas pictured in this book are from the following collections:

ABOUT THE AUTHORS

Ann Parker, photographer, (B.F.A. Yale University) and Avon Neal, writer, (M.F.A. Escuela de Bellas Artes, Mexico) are among the foremost folk art researchers and recorders working today. The Neals have been best known for their extensive work on New England gravestones for which they were awarded two Ford Foundation grants. Their extraordinary stone rubbings have been widely exhibited here and abroad and can be found in the permanent collections of more than 50 museums. Rubbings from Early New England Stone Sculpture, *a limited edition portfolio, was published in 1965.*

The Neals began a study of molas in the early 1960s while visiting the San Blas Islands. Many return trips to the islands, extensive research, and 17 years of experience in collecting molas have made them world authorities on the Cunas and this stunning stitchery. The Neals' work on molas, as well as other folk art forms, has appeared in Life, American Heritage, Art in America, The Smithsonian, *and* Americana. *Their book,* Ephemeral Folk Figures: Scarecrows, Harvest Figures, and Snowmen *was published by Clarkson N. Potter in 1969.*

When not traveling or lecturing, the Neals work and live in their 18th-century farmhouse in New England.

A NOTE ABOUT THE TYPE

The text of this book was set in photocomposition. The type-face selected is Palatino, designed in 1948 by the German typographer Hermann Zapf and issued between 1950 and 1952.

Named after Giovanbattista Palatino, a writing master of the Italian Renaissance, Palatino was the first of Zapf's typefaces to be introduced to America. Palatino is distinguished by broad letters and vigorous, inclined serifs typical of the work of a 16th-century Italian master of writing.

The display type is set in Tiffany. Tiffany is a dignified, graceful, superbly crafted type designed by the American typographer Ed Benguiat in four weights in 1972. The display type for this book was set in photodisplay in Tiffany Medium and Heavy.

The book was composed by The Monotype Composition Company, Baltimore, Maryland, and printed and bound by DNP (America), Inc., Japan.

The manuscript was edited by Carol Southern.

Production Supervision was by Michael Fragnito.

Typography and binding design by Hermann Strohbach.